Stately 'Gossip'

Stately 'Gossip'

 THE NATIONAL TRUST

First published by National Trust [Enterprises] Ltd
Copyright © Complete Editions 2005

Cover image courtesy of
Mary Evans Picture Library

Cover and design by Peter Wilkinson

Typesetting by David Onyett, Publishing & Production Services, Cheltenham

Manufactured in Thailand by Imago

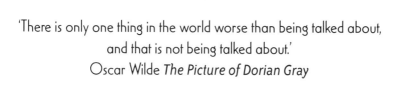

'There is only one thing in the world worse than being talked about, and that is not being talked about.'
Oscar Wilde *The Picture of Dorian Gray*

Stately 'Gossip'

INTRODUCTION

There is something about the private lives of the great and the good that is irresistible. Perhaps it is the chance to glimpse behind the usually serene exterior of stately homes and see how such people *really* live their lives that makes us so fascinated. Or maybe, secretly, we like to revel in the knowledge that while they may live in big houses, have servants, and know which fork to use for dinner, deep down baronets, barons, earls and even mighty dukes and duchesses are just the same as the rest of us – or even worse. Whatever the reason for our fascination, *Stately Gossip* is a veritable treasure trove of stories about how the 'other half' have led their lives. Whether it is the stories of the extraordinarily tangled love lives of dukes, the massive gambling debts of duchesses, or the plain simple daftness of eccentric old lords, this collection of stories sheds an amusing light on how the upper echelons have survived – or in some cases died out – over the past few hundreds of years.

Much of the best gossip, of course, has involved events that were supposed to stay strictly behind the doors of our wonderful stately homes, many of them now in the watchful hands of the National Trust. There is the story of the countess who tricked her errant lover into spending the night with a lowly and unattractive maid rather than his latest society beauty conquest. Or the lord who leapt into bed for some fun with his mistress only to discover he had gone into the wrong room and was instead rolling naked with a bishop.

Stately 'Gossip'

Another source of amusement and intrigue are the dinner and house parties so beloved of the owners of stately homes. Here, for example, we have the story of the drunken butler who insulted one of Britain's future prime ministers, or the guest who provoked the anger of the German military with a spoonful of frozen ice cream.

Money, sex, drink and power; they are all obsessions of the upper classes just as much as the rest of us, and all are reflected here. So sit back and enjoy these deliciously wicked stories that shine a humorous but merciless light on the world of stately homes, their guests — and of course their owners.

Stately 'Gossip'

The Ageing Bridegroom of Uppark

he elegant seventeenth-century house at Uppark, near Petersfield in West Sussex, has seen some interesting events and some extraordinary characters over the decades, but few people have been more outrageous than its former owner Sir Harry Featherstonhaugh, who lived there at the end of the eighteenth century and for the first half of the nineteenth. Sir Harry was very much his own man, and did things his way. In 1781 he took as his mistress a fifteen-year-old girl called Emily Lyon, much better known to us in history as the future Lady Hamilton and mistress of Horatio Nelson. Reprehensibly, Sir Harry banished her from Uppark when she became pregnant late that same year.

His next outrageous act was in 1810 when he told the Prince Regent, formerly a good friend, that he thought him a 'cad' and would have nothing more to do with him in the future. Admittedly some people might consider Sir Harry's judgement on the heir to the throne to have been a reasonable one.

The amorous Sir Harry's eventful life did not finish there. One day he heard a woman's voice singing in the dairy — a fine structure in its own right, designed by Humphry Repton — and asked to know whose it was. It belonged to the dairymaid's assistant, the appropriately named Mary Ann Bullock, and so smitten was Sir Harry with her that he asked her to marry him. Mary readily agreed and after a spell at a finishing school in Paris to prepare her for the demands of being mistress of a stately home, she married Sir Harry in 1825. At the time Mary was twenty-one — and Sir Harry was seventy. Despite their age difference, and though they had no children, the couple seem to have been happy enough. Sir Harry lived until 1846 when he had reached the grand old age of ninety-two — the end of a remarkable life.

The Rare Pear of Birr

angers can lie hidden in the most innocent visit to a stately home. That was certainly the experience of one visitor who had been invited to spend a weekend at the delightful Birr castle in County Offaly in the Irish Republic in the 1930s. Birr is the family home of Lord and Lady Rosse and boasts a number of fascinating features, including a giant telescope, known simply as the Great Telescope, and superb gardens packed full of rare and interesting plants. It also has the tallest box hedge in the world, standing at around thirty-six feet or eleven metres. Naturally excited at the prospect of a weekend in such beautiful surroundings, this guest arrived rather early and felt a little bit awkward at going up to the house before the hour at which he was expected.

So to kill a little time the gentleman decided to take a stroll around the garden. Given its beauty this was no hardship, and the guest, who was feeling a little hungry after his early start, even found something to sate his appetite, a pear growing on a rather elderly and unprepossessing pear tree. Having finished the fruit, the guest made his way towards the house from where he saw his hostess Lady Rosse, wife of the sixth Earl of Rosse, emerging. He tried to apologise for being a little early but the hospitable Lady Rosse would not hear of it. 'It's nothing to worry about,' said Lady Rosse, adding with a note of excitement, 'We're all going to see the pear'. It was now that the guest noted a veritable posse of visitors emerging from the house behind Lady Rosse and all heading determinedly towards the garden. He quickly learnt that they were an eminent group, too, experts in botany and horticulture from Britain and all over Europe, including experts in pear trees. One of the guests was even a specialist botanical artist who had been asked to do some detailed drawings. With a terrible sinking feeling our hapless visitor immediately realised just what it was that they had all come to see — *that* pear on the old pear tree. The pear, it seemed, was not just a rarity; it was the first time this particular tree had borne fruit in close to one hundred years. And after all those years of waiting, and with hordes of experts now arrived to examine this horticultural oddity, the early guest had simply walked up and eaten it.

For the scientific visitors it was a botanical blow of considerable proportions. For the unfortunate visitor, of course, it was a terrible reminder of what can befall even the most thoughtful of guests in stately homes.

Stately 'Gossip'

The Harpur Crewes of Calke

The early eighteenth-century Calke Abbey near Derby was the home for generations of some of Britain's most eccentric aristocrats, the Harpur Crewe family. When the 5th Baronet Sir Harry, who was born in 1708, married Lady Caroline Manners, they received a fine wedding present from the royal family: a four-poster bed complete with exquisite Chinese silk. But the expensive bed was never used or even unwrapped – possibly because the rooms at the Abbey were too low to incorporate its extreme size.

Later down the years the 9th Baronet Sir John helped start Calke Abbey's collection of stuffed animals, a collection that can still be seen to this day at this National Trust-run property. Sir John was also something of a recluse, his visitor book at the house recording not a single entry during one twenty-year period in the nineteenth century.

But the oddest member of the family was probably the 10th Baronet Sir Vauncy Harpur Crewe who inherited the property in 1886. He, too, was a collector of stuffed birds and animals – and was also very reclusive. He refused to talk to his servants, relaying his instructions instead by letter, and would apparently head for the safety of the woods if ever his wife had invited guests. Sir Vauncy also disliked the then newly invented motor cars and forbade them to enter his land.

Stately 'Gossip'

On another occasion he supposedly had a hill blown up with gunpowder simply because he did not like the view.

Drunk as a Lord

The wonderfully named Clotworthy John Skeffington rejoiced in the even more exotic noble titles of the 11th Viscount Massereene and the 4th Viscount Ferrard, often shortened to the Viscount Massereene and Ferrard. Perhaps it was because of the colourful nature of his names, but the viscount, born in 1842, was an equally colourful character who was very often the worse for wear thanks to his drinking habits. His loyal wife Florence, who nowadays would be described as 'long suffering', spent most of their marriage trying to reduce her husband's boozing, or at least lessen the effects of it. However, he was a cunning and ingenious man and often evaded her well-meaning attempts to keep him on the path of righteousness. The Viscount's frequent excessive drinking led to a popular saying at the time: 'There goes Lord Massereene and Ferrard and they're both drunk.'

It seems that the Viscount himself was aware of this amusing joke at his expense, even if it did little to curb his ways. One evening he was making his way unsteadily down a street in Mayfair when he was approached by a police constable. 'Good evening sir,' said the constable to the staggering figure. 'Can you tell me your name?' he asked, knowing there was a fair chance that the inebriated man might not be able to remember it. 'Massereene and Ferrard,' said the drunken man. 'Both drunk.' And with that his lordship weaved off into the night.

The Toffee Incident of Polesden Lacey

The estate of Polesden Lacey has one of the best views of any land in southern England, sitting as it does on the North Downs at Great Bookham, near Dorking. It was also once a byword for elegant and very exclusive dinner parties and weekend parties held for the amusement of the cream of British society. The reason for this was its redoubtable hostess the Hon Mrs Ronald Greville, who in the early part of the twentieth century was one of the best-connected figures in the country. Through her husband she was a good friend of Edward VII, and indeed the future George VI and his new bride Elizabeth (the late Queen Mother) stayed at Polesden for part of their honeymoon. As well as royalty, heads of state, politicians, aristocrats, writers, artists and playwrights were among the regular guests at the estate. The house — now run by the National Trust — was also brim full of fine works of art and furniture, while her dinners were noted for their excellent French cuisine, all a tribute to Mrs Greville's exquisite taste.

So it was that a formidable group of guests gathered at the house one evening, looking forward to an exquisite meal and sparkling conversation. The party, which included the Earl of Oxford and

Stately 'Gossip'

Asquith and the writer A.P. Herbert, were about to make their way into dinner when Mrs Greville – a widow after her husband died in 1908 – confided in one guest that she was having to 'make do' with the sous chef as the main chef was unwell and unable to cook that night. However, this made little difference to the quality of the food, as the diners made their way through course after course, and the conversation flowed as agreeably as the wine. It seemed to be yet another dinner party triumph for the pre-eminent hostess of the day.

Suddenly, however, a hush descended on the guests for no immediately obvious reason. Then all became clear. They had been silenced not by some controversial or outrageous remark – but by the dessert. It appears that when Mrs Greville had instructed the sous chef to make a chocolate mousse with coffee sauce, he had misheard this as 'toffee' sauce. As a consequence all the diners' teeth were gummed up with this tough, chewy and inedible dessert.

Cheers for Chatsworth

Chatsworth House in Derbyshire, which is still the home of the Dukes of Devonshire, used to make its own beer. The refreshing beverage was pumped a few hundred yards from the brewery through piping down to the house cellar, where it was then stored in vast 100-gallon barrels for later consumption by the household and servants. This pumping operation took place once every two weeks.

Stately 'Gossip'

In the 1950s the lead piping through which the beer passed was dug up and replaced, partly for health and safety reasons and partly for the scrap value of the lead. It was during this work that a curious discovery was made. Along one section of the pipe had been fixed an extra tap. Further examination revealed that this tap fed a subsidiary pipe that led straight to the nearby gardeners' quarters, where at the time the more than fifty estate gardeners lived. It appeared that every fortnight someone in the gardeners' residence had opened the tap to appropriate part of the beer as it was being pumped through to the Chatsworth cellar. This now explained the unusual rowdiness and noise that used to come from those rooms every time a delivery of beer was made, and also why for one morning each fortnight the gardening standards at Chatsworth were not up to their normal immaculate standards.

Lord of the Ring

George Nathaniel Curzon, the 1st Marquess Curzon of Kedleston, and the son of the 4th Baron Scarsdale, rector of Kedleston, was one of the grandest as well as one of the most brilliant men of his generation. Indeed, while he was still a student at Balliol College, Oxford, some lines were written about him that seemed to sum up much of his approach to life. These were:

'My name is George Nathaniel Curzon, I am a most superior person.

Stately 'Gossip'

'My cheek is pink, my hair is sleek, I dine at Blenheim once a week.'

Given such sentiments it is perhaps not wholly surprising to learn how this mighty intellectual and political heavyweight could sometimes be out of touch with the way 'ordinary' people lived. The great man was once walking down Regent Street with a friend when they stopped to admire some jewellery in a shop window. As they were examining the glittering display Curzon pointed at an object and asked his friend, 'What's that?'

His friend followed Curzon's gaze and saw that he was looking at a small silver ring-like object. 'That,' said the friend, 'is a napkin ring.'

'A "napkin ring"?' queried Curzon. 'What on earth is a napkin ring?'

To which his friend replied, 'Surely you know what a napkin ring is for?'

'No I do not,' responded Curzon. 'What does it do?'

His friend explained patiently that not everyone could afford to have fresh linen for their napkins at every meal, and that after breakfast people would fold their napkin, push it through a silver napkin ring like the one in the window and then use the napkin again at lunch.

Stately 'Gossip'

Curzon shook his head in wonderment and disbelief. 'Can there really be such poverty?' he asked.

Escape from Fonthill

William Beckford , who was born in 1760, and who was just about the wealthiest man in Britain in his day, was a brilliant collector of art and lived at Fonthill, a magnificent estate not far from Bath. All this should have made Beckford one of the most popular men in the country. Instead he came to be shunned by just about all of 'polite' society, was the subject of the most vicious gossip and was refused a peerage by George III, who apparently let it be known he would have liked to see the man hanged instead.

The cause of this remarkable antipathy towards Beckford was that as a teenager he had fallen in love with a young boy, nine years his junior, called the Hon William Courtenay, later 3rd Viscount and 9th Earl of Devon whose family home was at Powderham Castle, near Exeter. At first their friendship passed without great comment but one day a visitor at Powderham claimed to hear strange noises emanating from the boy's bedroom and the youngster was supposedly found in bed with Beckford.

The great scandal involving William Beckford and his friend 'Kitty' – as Courtenay was dubbed – had started and not even the former's enormous wealth could save him from being ostracised. For a while

Stately 'Gossip'

Beckford went to live in Portugal, away from gossiping tongues, but even when he returned years later he was still shunned by society. Instead Beckford decided to erect a huge wall around his estate, topped with iron spikes, to confirm his new life as a virtual recluse from society. (It also stopped hunters getting in and killing the estate's animals, for Beckford was very fond of wildlife.) Meanwhile Beckford devoted much of his life to an ambitious building project at Fonthill and to collecting art, though both combined to whittle away his fortune.

Safe within the walls of Fonthill the very talented but unpredictable Beckford displayed a macabre, even cruel, sense of humour. On one occasion a young man made his way through the estate's defences and found himself in a vegetable plot where a man was digging vegetables. The 'gardener' asked why the young man was there, and on being told that he had heard about the splendour of Fonthill and wanted to see it for himself, the gardener gave the intruder a tour of the gardens and greenhouses, and then of the house itself. It was only then that the 'gardener' revealed to the young man that he was William Beckford and urged the guest to stay for dinner. The young man readily agreed and enjoyed a fine meal and long conversations with the reclusive estate owner. At eleven pm Beckford went off to bed, and the butler showed the young guest to the front door.

The loyal retainer passed on Beckford's compliments and added, 'I am to say that as you made your way into Fonthill Abbey without assistance, you may find your way out again as best you can, and he hopes that you take care to avoid the bloodhounds that are let into the gardens every night. Good evening sir.'

With that the butler closed the door and the terrified young man was left alone in the dark. He quickly climbed up the nearest tree to avoid the dogs and spent the night there, before making his way out the next morning, a puzzled and chastened uninvited guest.

The Bills of Blenheim

Sir John Vanbrugh, the architect who designed the magnificent Blenheim Palace, discovered that when it comes to paying their bills the aristocracy can be as bad as anyone. Sir John once moaned to a friend that he felt he had little chance of ever getting the £2,000 he felt he was owed for his troubles, thanks to that 'wicked woman of Marlborough' – a reference to the Duchess of Marlborough. He noted that the Duchess had even tried to get a debt owed by the Duke to workmen for other work passed on to him, Sir John. 'For which I think she ought to be hanged,' he added angrily.

The Duchess naturally had friends in high places and even succeeded in getting an injunction from no less a legal figure than her friend the Lord Chancellor, stating that Vanbrugh had never worked for the Duke and had no claims on the estate. Her approach to paying 'tradespeople' was summed up in a letter she wrote to her daughter about a foreman, one Mr Wood: 'Painters, poets and builders have very high flights but they must be kept down … You will not forget to make a bargain with Mr Wood since most people, as well as he, are apt to overvalue their works.'

The Proud Duke

The 6th Duke of Somerset Charles Seymour only succeeded to the dukedom in 1678 because his brother Francis was killed by an Italian named Horatio Botti. The 5th Duke had allegedly insulted the Genoese gentleman's wife and in revenge the slighted gentleman had shot the English nobleman.

Perhaps the unexpectedness of inheriting the title explains some of Charles Seymour's curious behaviour, though this may have been due more to the enormous pride he took in his family and its nobility. For example, he refused to talk to his servants and instead communicated with them in sign language. The Duke, who was incidentally also very proud of his good looks, had houses built beside his routes into London so that he could avoid staying in inns along the way – presumably so he did not have to mix with common people or waste his wonderful features on their unworthy gaze.

The 'proud duke' as he was also dubbed could be as unforgiving with his family. He instructed one of his daughters to keep an eye on him after dinner when he took his nap, in case he should fall off his chair or couch. One day his daughter was distracted by something and the slumbering Duke duly fell off. The punishment for this 'crime' was that the Duke refused to speak to his daughter for a whole year.

The Canal Duke

The 3rd Duke of Bridge, Francis Egerton, was known as the 'Canal Duke' thanks to his interest in water and engineering. The Duke, born in 1736, and who succeeded to his title at the age of eleven, was keen to exploit the coal under the ground of his estates at Worsley near Manchester. To do this he needed to have some way of transporting the material, and having been on tours of France and Italy the Duke was impressed by the usefulness of canals he had seen there. Accordingly an expert, James Brindley, was called in to help design and supervise the project.

One of the most striking structures in the canal was the Barton Aqueduct. This took the canal nearly forty feet in the air over the River Irwell. An admirer at the time described it romantically as a 'castle in the air'. The Duke's aqueduct was a popular local landmark but was sadly destroyed in 1894 to make way for the Manchester Ship Canal.

The Duke's passion for engineering was not matched by a love of the natural world. Though he had plenty of space at his Worsley home he refused to have shrubs or even flowers growing there. Once while he was away someone planted some flowers in a misguided attempt to please his lordship. Upon his return an angry Duke smashed off their heads with his stick and ordered that all their roots should be dug up as well. It is not entirely clear why Egerton was so against growing decorative plants on his land. One theory is that he simply saved money by not having to employ an army of gardeners constantly to be maintaining the grounds. Another is that flowers formed an association with something bad from his past, perhaps the unhappy end to a love affair.

Certainly his grace had nursed a broken heart after his attempts in the 1750s to marry a beautiful Irish woman called Elizabeth Gunning fell through. (At the time she was the widow of a duke and later married another duke so she did not herself miss out on the joys of high society.) In fact he was so upset at the incident and with the female of the species in general that he henceforward refused even to be waited upon by a woman.

However, the more prosaic and more likely reason for his dislike of ornamental plants is that the Duke only valued objects that were useful and as far as he was concerned flowers and shrubs served no practical purpose.

Stately 'Gossip'

The Unflappable Butler

The 18th Baron Dunsany, otherwise know as Edward John Moreton Drax Plunkett, was a remarkable man who possessed genuine ability as a chess player, wrote chess puzzles for *The Times*, was a patron of the arts, a keen cricketer and by all accounts was a fine shot too. Above all, he was an acclaimed writer and playwright. The baron's home was the impressive Dunsany Castle in County Meath, in Ireland, whose construction was begun in the twelfth century and where the family butler seemed to have picked up some of his lordship's dramatic timing. On one occasion the armed force known as the Black and Tans — the nickname for a special auxiliary force of the Royal Irish Constabulary used to combat Sinn Fein in the early 1920s — abruptly paid a visit to Dunsany. Not noted for their tact and discretion, they soon created something of a mess as they quickly searched the area. At their equally abrupt departure the butler gently enquired of the soldiers, 'Who shall I say called?'

To Bore or Not to Bore

The 1st Earl of Dudley John William Ward, who served as British Foreign Secretary from 1827 to 1828, was a man of learning as well as a politician, but also possessed some endearingly eccentric traits. Many of us rehearse imminent conversations with other people in our minds, but Ward, who was

Stately 'Gossip'

also the 4th Viscount Dudley and Ward, practised these conversations out loud. This occasionally led to embarrassment, for example on the occasion when he was presenting a country squire at court. The event had passed without hitch until the pair were leaving the palace together in a carriage. Even in those pre-car days London could suffer traffic jams, and their carriage soon became well and truly trapped in a sea of other vehicles. It was then that the Earl, who was sitting next to the country squire, began to rehearse the impending scenario. 'Now this tiresome country squire will be expecting me to ask him to dine,' mused the Earl out loud. 'Shall I? Or shall I not? On the whole I think not,' he concluded. 'I think he might be a bore.'

Naturally the squire was somewhat taken aback at these remarks, and for a moment was rendered speechless. But being a quick-witted soul himself, he looked out at the traffic jam and mused out loud, 'Now this tiresome old peer will of course be asking me to dine with him today. Shall I or shall I not? No. I am pretty sure it would be a bore.'

For a moment there was a strained silence, before the Earl saw the funny and courageous side of his companion's remarks and with genuine sincerity asked the squire to dine with him.

Stately 'Gossip'

The Madman of Renishaw Hall

Splendid Renishaw Hall in Derbyshire has been in the Sitwell family for three and a half centuries and its much praised Italianate gardens were created by Sir George Reresby Sitwell, the father of Edith, Osbert and Sacheverell ('Sachie') Sitwell. Sir George was something of an eccentric and alas even the many attractions of Renishaw could not always entertain him.

Having once banished all guests from the house on a whim – he suddenly felt unsocial – he then complained of boredom. He told his son Osbert that he would like to go on holiday in a nice country hotel in a quiet spot with fine views, privacy and a few entertaining guests with whom to chat. Osbert said he had seen just the very place advertised in a newspaper only that morning. So the son and rest of the family encouraged Sir George to book a month's break in this enticing establishment, leaving Sir George's secretary to make the reservation. The booking confirmation duly arrived, but unfortunately the owners of the establishment rather gave away the surprise that lay in store for Sir George. The 'hotel's' manager had written: 'Ought a straitjacket to be sent for Sir George to wear during the journey? Three strong and practised male nurses will of course be in attendance and prepared to quell any disturbance.'

For what the family had unaccountably neglected to tell Sir George was that he had been booked to stay a month in an expensive private institution for the mentally deranged.

The Naked Truth

Opening stately homes to visitors is nothing new. Wilton House in Wiltshire, the home of the Earl of Pembroke, was proudly shown off to noble visitors in the eighteenth century. The then earl even had a guide book produced.

Occasionally though his zeal for showing off the magnificent house and its contents backfired on him. He once decided to add a little colour to the faces and eyes of some of his many statues, to make them even more lifelike. So happy was the earl with his handiwork that he immediately rushed off to collect some female guests who were in the house, to show them the effect. Returning with the ladies, the Earl ushered them into the room where the statues stood, exclaiming, 'Walk in ladies, it is life itself.' Unfortunately the ladies got rather more life than either they or the Earl had bargained for. During his absence some nameless youth in the house had decided to add the colour to more intimate parts of the male and female statues, the results of which were all too evident as the Earl's companions stared at their naked forms.

Stately 'Gossip'

Hellgate: The Outrageous Earl of Barrymore

The family of the Earls of Barrymore seems to have produced more than its share of curious characters at the end of the eighteenth century. The short-lived Richard Barry, 7th Earl of Barrymore had a nickname that summed up his approach to life – Hellgate. Meanwhile his brother Henry, who became the 8th Earl on Richard's death in 1794, had possessed a dodgy leg from birth and was cruelly called Cripplegate. Another brother, the Honorable and Reverend Augustus Barry, was apparently even more of a dissolute character than the other two and earned the nickname Newgate. This was supposedly the only jail in the country he had not been thrown into. Not to be outdone, their sister Lady Milfort was also given a nickname. The Prince Regent apparently called her Billingsgate on account of her colourful use of language.

Yet it was Richard, the 7th Earl, who was the most extraordinary character of all of them. During his life he is said to have spent a staggering £300,000, chiefly on buying and setting up two theatres – drama was a great passion of his – and on betting and keeping horses. He was a good swordsman and boxer, and had his own personal boxer, by the name of Hooper the Tinman, who also doubled up as a bodyguard – a necessary asset for a man who liked to visit the roughest parts of London and get into arguments.

Stately 'Gossip'

Richard Barry was addicted to gambling, and used to take up the most outrageous bets. He once made a bet that he could beat a man on horseback over a hundred-yard course with a turn around a tree in the middle. Even after four heats the result apparently was a tie.

His betting and other passions constantly meant he was having to dodge creditors — even after his death. He was killed tragically young when he dropped a loaded gun in his carriage and it went off, shooting him through the eye. Afraid that people to whom he owed money would seize the corpse against payment of debts, Barry's friends moved his body at night to be buried at Wargrave in Berkshire where the 7th Earl had lived. It was a fittingly absurd end to an absurd life. Ironically, once Barry's chaotic financial arrangements were sorted out after his death, it was discovered that his assets in fact exceeded his debts.

After Dinner Shooting

They say an Englishman's home is his castle, and this is equally true whether the home in question is a terraced house, a bungalow or even a stately home. The principle is the same; the house must be defended to the last against the enemy, real or imagined.

That was certainly the view of the grand if rather impetuous Earl of Milnthorpe who was enjoying a sumptuous dinner with his guests at Dallam Tower in Cumbria in the early part of the nineteenth century.

Stately 'Gossip'

Having partaken well of the food, and especially the wine, Lord Milnthorpe was regaling his co-diners with stories on the terrace when he thought he saw a shadowy figure in the evening gloom. It was, the nobleman reasoned, almost certainly a poacher, and poachers needed to be taught a lesson. In a flash his lordship had got up and run to where he stored his guns, chosen a likely gun and run back to the terrace.

The guests pleaded with Milnthorpe to put down his firearm, doubtless fearing the embarrassment or worse if the aristocrat managed to 'bag' a poacher in front of them. But Lord Milnthorpe was not a man who was easily deterred, and he raised his gun to his shoulder and fired with a terrific bang, a noise followed quickly by an almighty crash. It seemed his lordship had hit his target, but oddly there was no cry of pain from the victim.

With mounting anxiety some of the braver guests went out to investigate what had happened and to see who or what the nobleman had actually hit. The answer lay on the ground before them. For the well-oiled Lord Milnthorpe had spied not a poacher in the darkness but one of the eighteenth-century statues that adorned the grounds outside his home. And the peer had managed to hit the stone figure a direct hit on its head, which now lay in shattered pieces all about. The guests chuckled with relief and amusement; after all, it was the kind of mistake that any chap could make – especially after such a fine dinner.

Stately 'Gossip'

Loyal Mistress

n the past, the mistress of an aristocrat or even a royal duke would often transfer their loyalty to another lover when circumstances dictated, or a better position became available. An exception was Madame St Laurent, who for twenty-seven years was the loyal and devoted mistress of the Duke of Kent. When eventually the Duke was prevailed upon to marry and provide a future heir to the throne, Madame St Laurent did not switch her affections to another powerful person. Instead, so upset was she and so loyal to the Duke, that she chose to retire to a convent for the rest of her days. The Duke also did his duty; he married Victoria, the Princess of Leiningen, and their daughter was Queen Victoria.

In the Soup

he elegant Hoar Cross Hall in Staffordshire, which is now an acclaimed health spa, was for many generations the family home of the Meynell family. Lady Dorothy Meynell, the daughter of a duke and who married Colonel Francis Meynell, was fond of holding court at lavish dinner parties at this mid-nineteenth-century hall.

Regrettably Lady Dorothy had an unfortunate 'affliction' by which small droplets of moisture would form on the end of her nose during dinner. To ensure that such droplets could be swiftly detected and disposed of, her ladyship had devised a cunning plan with her butler. Whenever the trusty retainer noticed one of the habitual droplets forming on his mistress's nose, he was to inform her 'Roger's at the door'.

To any guest this would sound an innocent remark concerning perhaps an errand boy or another member of the staff who needed her attention. Only the two of them knew what the message really meant. This plan generally worked well enough, giving her ladyship time and opportunity to depart to the ladies' room to powder her nose.

The problem was that as an inveterate and determined conversationalist, her ladyship could not always be relied on to react immediately to the butler's warning signal. During one dinner party Lady Dorothy became so engrossed in the story she was telling that she was completely oblivious to the butler's promptings. As soon as he had noticed a droplet forming the butler had given the agreed warning, 'Roger's at the door' but to no avail. Three times the butler gave the signal —'Roger's at the door' — each time more urgently than the last, yet each time Lady Dorothy failed to take heed even though her nose was reaching crisis point. Finally the exasperated butler was forced to announce in a very loud voice that everyone present could hear, 'Roger's in the soup, Milady!'

Stately 'Gossip'

The Duke of Steaks

The 11th Duke of Norfolk Charles Howard was known as the 'Drunken Duke' and he certainly enjoyed the odd drink or two. But the duke was also equally fond of food and plenty of it. He was a member of an elite dining club at the end of the eighteenth century called 'The Sublime Society of Beef Steaks', where Howard and others from the upper social echelons ate vast quantities of beef.

The club was formed as a reaction against 'fancy' French food at the time; even champagne and French wine were avoided in favour of punch. On one memorable occasion the duke is said to have started a meal with some fish and then proceeded to eat no fewer than fifteen giant steaks. Unsurprisingly this mammoth meal lasted from three o'clock in the afternoon until past midnight. Yet despite his decidedly unhealthy eating and drinking habits the 11th Duke lived until 1815 having reached the respectable age of sixty-nine.

Night Time Reading

Lord Harrowby of yesteryear had an unfortunate way of entertaining guests at his impressive family home at Sandon near Stafford – he liked to read to them after dinner. On one occasion he read non-stop for three-and-a-half hours, an experience that seems to have been too much even for the Earl's wife. The Countess of Granville wrote of the evening: 'I see Lady Harrowby in such a fidget that she can hardly keep from screaming.'

The Boozy Butler of Luton Hoo

The diamond magnate Sir Julius Wernher and his wife Lady Wernher were known to give the most exquisite dinner parties at both their home in Piccadilly and also their country house, Luton Hoo in Bedfordshire, a grand building designed by Robert Adam for the Earl of Bute in the eighteenth century.

It was hardly a surprise that their dinner parties were so fine. Sir Julius, as well as being fabulously rich, was a well-known connoisseur of the fine arts and a noted collector. Lady Wernher, meanwhile, born Alice Sedgwick Mankiewicz and usually known as 'Birdie', was very musical and noted for her own good taste and for her ability to throw a good party. When the couple married in 1889 it was a match made in heaven.

One evening the couple were entertaining guests who included the young Winston Churchill. Even when a young man it was clear he would go far one day and Sir Julius had an eye for up and coming talent in politics as well as in art.

The dinner party was, as usual, going fine; perhaps too well in fact as most of the guests were becoming quite drunk, including Churchill.

Even worse, though, was the growing realisation by 'Birdie' that her butler was even more drunk than the rest of them. This fact was impressed upon her when he managed to pour some sauce all over her dress.

Deciding that this situation had gone on long enough Lady Wernher dashed off a quick note, which she then slipped to the butler when next he lurched past. It read 'You are drunk. Leave the room at once.' The butler stared at the note for a second, whereupon he placed it carefully on a silver platter and marched unsteadily to the other end of the table and presented it to a bemused Winston Churchill.

Tactless at Taplow

Lord Desborough, previously known as William or W.H. Grenfell, was a well-known sportsman. In particular he was a fine fisherman and was reputed to be one of the best shots in England before the First World War. He and his wife Lady Desborough – born Ethel or 'Ettie' Fane – lived at Taplow Court, built in 1855, in Buckinghamshire.

The large house was at the time littered with trophies testifying to his lordship's prowess as a sportsman. (It is now a cultural centre for a Buddhist organisation.) And like many a sporting man, he also had something of an eye for the women, despite his own apparently happy marriage to Lady Desborough. This explains why during one weekend house party the great adventurer decided to take a young woman by the name of Miss Fisher out for a punt on the river.

Miss Fisher was by all accounts a very attractive young woman, though doubtless Lord Desborough simply wanted to show off his ability at punting. Now perhaps he showed off too much, or maybe the river bed was especially tricky in that area, but in any case disaster soon struck. The pole got caught in the bottom of the river and Lord Desborough plunged headlong into the waters. For an eminent sportsman such as himself, this was something of a humiliation; it was bad enough falling in the river, but to do this in front of a young woman made it far, far worse.

After swearing his attractive young companion to secrecy, Lord Desborough tried to make his way discreetly back into the house unseen in order to dry off, but his alas bedraggled figure was spotted by another guest who promptly informed Lady Desborough of what he had seen.

Her ladyship immediately guessed what had happened and knew what she had to do. Later that day she confronted Miss Fisher and to the young woman's astonishment accused her of having pushed her blameless husband into the river.

It was pointless Miss Fisher trying to protest her innocence, for Lady Desborough had quite made up her mind. Lord Desborough was such an accomplished sportsman that he could *only* have fallen in the river if he had been pushed. There was also the small matter of wanting to get rid of a house guest in whom Lord Desborough had clearly taken a close interest. So it was that poor young Miss Fisher was forced to return to London, where she was known for some time as the woman who had 'ducked Desborough'.

Lord Saye and the Sherry

The Lords of Saye and Sele, who have been associated with Broughton Castle in Oxfordshire, have a colourful past. According to the Regency commentator Captain Gronow, one forebear of the dynasty – whose family name is Fiennes – was noted for his taste in food and alcohol. At one breakfast he served an omelette that consisted solely of golden pheasants' eggs. Meanwhile his lordship could happily swig away on absinthe and curacao with no discernible impact on his state of sobriety. Once when his lordship was going out for dinner his servant asked if he had any orders for him. 'Place two bottles of sherry by my bedside and call me the day after tomorrow,' came the reply.

The Chequered Past of Claydon House

The undoubted and understandable desire of many aristocrats to live in the grandest possible house can sometimes lead to their undoing. Such a cautionary tale involves the fascinating character of Ralph 2nd Earl Verney, whose family had settled at Claydon House at Middle Claydon in Buckinghamshire.

Ralph Verney was determined to have a family home worthy of his family name and, as importantly, to match or surpass that of a political rival, the Earl Temple, who was at the time using his vast fortune to redesign the magnificent stately home of Stowe. Alas Earl Verney lacked Temple's huge wealth and was hopeless with money, except at spending it. His clever but unscrupulous architect Luke Lightfoot ended up defrauding his client, taking the money for expensive materials but using cheaper ones on the house and pocketing the difference. When the affair eventually came to court it transpired that out of £30,000 that Verney thought had been spent on building the house, only £7,000 had ultimately been used to that end. The rest had been siphoned off by Lightfoot. Much of the building work was beautiful but ultimately this was to be of limited comfort to Ralph Verney. His poor handling of finance and the exorbitant cost of the building work eventually led him into bankruptcy and in the honoured tradition of the time he fled to France and into exile as a debtor.

There is a sad footnote to this already sad story. In 1771 Verney secretly came back to the deserted Claydon House to see his 'creation'. A young stable lad peered through the cobwebbed windows and saw the Earl shambling through the empty echoing corridors of the great house. Two thirds of the house were pulled down just twenty years after it was rebuilt, though now the structure has been lovingly restored by the National Trust. At least Verney's dream was one day realised even if he had died, penniless, many years before.

An Ungrateful Napoleon

Marguerite, Countess of Blessington, was a rare figure in British society in the first half of the nineteenth century, a woman and member of the aristocracy who wrote for money. This practical streak probably came from her tough upbringing in a large and poor family in Tipperary in Ireland, where she was born plain Sally Power. Eventually her extraordinary beauty and matching intelligence drew her into the upper circles of British society and she married Lord Blessington in 1818. Even then her life was tough by the standards of many around her, as her husband's excessive spending and then his death obliged her to earn a living of her own, by writing. Eventually, late in life, she was forced to flee to Paris to escape her debts, though she never lost her beauty or her intelligence and razor sharp wit, as she showed in an encounter with the French president of the day.

Years before, the future Napoleon III of France had been a regular visitor to Lady Blessington's London salon when the Frenchman was getting over the failure of an attempted coup in his own country, the first of two failed coups that led him to exile. Now, however,

Stately 'Gossip'

Napoleon was president of France and felt it would be displeasing to meet a woman who reminded him of past failures and his periods of exile. The debt-ridden Lady Blessington was determined to renew their acquaintance and managed to engineer a meeting with the president at a Paris reception.

'Greetings, Lady Blessington,' said an embarrassed Napoleon. 'Will you be staying in France for some time?'

Lady Blessington curtsied her acknowledgement that she would be, and then replied with a smile to the French head of state, 'And you?'

And One's Name is . . .?

The Earls of Portarlington, a distinguished line of the Irish nobility, have had a colourful past, if not always an entirely happy one. The 2nd Earl was considered to be in disgrace after he was late joining his regiment the 23rd Regiment of Light Dragoons just before Waterloo; it was not the kind of regiment or the kind of battle one kept waiting.

Then there is the marvellous story of the 5th Earl's performance at a gathering in which royalty was to be present. Portarlington George Lionel Henry Seymour Dawson-Damer, to give him his other names, had apparently been well 'refreshed' by the time that it was his turn to meet a member of the Royal Family. Now, we can all get confused on occasions, especially when one has had the odd glass or two to drink. But at such times most of us are wise enough to keep quiet until the moment has passed. Not so poor Lord Portarlington who, mystified by the female figure in front of him, uttered the memorable words, 'Damn it, Ma'am, I know your face but I cannot put a name to it' to the reigning monarch of Great Britain, her many colonies and the Empress of India, Queen Victoria herself.

One can be confident in saying that, on this occasion at least, Her Majesty was most definitely not amused.

Dismay in Dunster

There has been a fortified building on the site of the wonderfully located Dunster Castle in Somerset since Norman times, and for many centuries it was occupied by the Luttrell family, before being passed on to the National Trust.

One day in the early 1960s the then incumbent, Geoffrey Luttrell – a respected former diplomat and then a company director – was travelling by train back up to London. In the same compartment were two women of a certain age who had obviously just been on holiday in the resort of Minehead, which is close to Dunster. As they passed Dunster Castle one of the women asked the other if she had managed to visit the place. Upon learning that her companion had not made it – thanks to 'the weather' – the first woman began extolling the virtues of the castle and its gardens, much to the quiet delight of Geoffrey Luttrell as he sat reading his newspaper.

He suddenly had reason to listen more intently, however, when he heard the woman add, 'That's why it's all so tragic.' Luttrell now peered over his newspaper in time to see the woman holding her finger to her temple and slowly circling it, indicating what was apparently wrong. 'There's a husband, wife and two children, all the same apparently,' she sighed. 'Such a shame.'

Controversial Cliveden

Cliveden in Berkshire is the nineteenth-century stately home that became the centre of much of British political and society activity in the twentieth century. Cliveden was the home of Nancy, Lady Astor, who in 1919 became the first woman to take up a seat in the House of Commons. In time the circle of powerful friends and acquaintances who visited the place for lavish house parties became known as the 'Cliveden Set'.

In 1961 the house – which is now owned by the National Trust and let as a five star hotel – achieved notoriety when it was the venue for the events of the Profumo Affair. The Cabinet minister John Profumo had a brief liaison with a showgirl called Christine Keeler, whom he first met at Cliveden; she was apparently lying naked by the swimming pool at the time. The affair would have counted for little but for the fact that Profumo was the Secretary of State for War and it emerged that Keeler also had a relationship with a naval attaché at the Soviet Embassy in London, Yevgeny Ivanov. Profumo later resigned and devoted his subsequent career to charitable works.

The Wrong Kind of Ice Cream

Houghton Hall, which lies in Norfolk close to the coast, is a magnificent stately home with a rich history. It was here that Sir Robert Walpole, who was Britain's first prime minister, lived and used to entertain his guests after a tough day's hunting on the extensive estate.

The Hall, for many generations the family home of the Cholmondeleys, was also the scene of a bizarre dinner party in the early part of the twentieth century. It was August 1914 and already fairly clear to most diplomatic observers that a bitter war in Europe was coming and that Britain, a country that had enjoyed relative peace — at least on her doorstep — for so long, would be thrust to the centre stage of this conflict. Nonetheless, there was still time for a fine dinner party given by the Hall's host the 4th Marquess of Cholmondeley. Moreover two of the guests for the evening were German army officers. Though all knew that war was coming, their presence was a sign that for now at least the outward symbols of civilised behaviour could still be maintained. Yet it was a strained occasion, the conversation was polite but guarded and most of those present felt a sense of tension pervading the atmosphere.

However, the evening passed without incident until dessert arrived , a rather well-frozen lump of ice cream. One of the guests was a youthful John Masterman, later vice-chancellor of Oxford University and who was to work with British Intelligence in the Second World War. Masterman decided to tackle the hard ice cream head on and lunged at it with his spoon, only for the rock-like dessert to fly off his dish and straight down the rather ample cleavage of one of the German officer's wives sitting opposite him. There was a split second of awed silence while everyone subconsciously absorbed the awfulness of what had just happened, before the two German officers leapt to their feet as one. The aggrieved spouse accused Masterman of deliberately insulting his wife by flicking the ice cream at her and said that were the academic a military man he would demand 'satisfaction'. As it was, he warned ominously, 'We will soon find out whether you British are as cowardly as you are ill-mannered!'

With that the two officers and their partners left the room. Again there was a split second of silence as no one quite knew how to react to this dreadful situation. The silence was broken by the host, the Marquess of Cholmondeley, who jovially remarked, 'Good shot Masterman — that will teach those Bosch a lesson, eh?' before returning to his dessert.

Stately *'Gossip'*

Wooing at Warwick Castle

Warwick Castle is considered by many to be one of the finest castles in England, and has witnessed many historic moments ever since William the Conqueror created the Earldom of Warwick to keep a watchful eye on the region.

At the end of the nineteenth century and start of the twentieth it was also the scene of some very fine house parties under the tolerant eye of Lady Warwick. It was not unknown for romantic and illicit liaisons to flourish in such circumstances, though in the case of the ageing Comtesse d'Harcourt, this was not always desirable. She was staying at the castle with her beau Lord William Seagrave in the summer of 1895 when his eye was caught by an attractive and much younger woman by the name of Celia Dunnett, an American from Massachusetts. As was his wont, Lord William decided to make a conquest of the young woman and fixed a plan to visit her room in the night when everyone else in the house would be — or at least should have been — asleep.

Alas for him their romantic discussion was overheard by none other than the Comtesse herself. Naturally distraught at coming second best to another woman, and a younger one at that, she wisely decided to get even, not mad. Among the details she had overheard was that the delectable Miss Dunnett would leave a rose outside her door to indicate to Lord William which was her room as he crept along the dark corridor. The Comtesse quickly hatched a plan and kept watch late that evening on Miss Dunnett's room which, handily, was close to her own. As soon as she saw the rose appear on her young rival's door, the Comtesse picked the flower up and placed it outside the door of the least attractive maid in the house.

It is unkindly said by some that Lord William went ahead with the late night liaison and yet never realised his mistake; though whether this is being unkind to Lord William or to Miss Dunnett is a moot point.

The Woman with Three Fathers

he personal circumstances of Maria-Emily Fagniani were extraordinary even by the fairly relaxed standards of the upper classes at the end of the eighteenth century. Her mother was a notable beauty of the day, the Marchesa Fagniani. But as to exactly who her father was, no one seemed to be sure. No fewer than three rich, powerful and well-connected men claimed her as their daughter. The first was the Marchese Fagniani himself, the second was George Augustus Selwyn, MP, society wit and notorious womaniser of his day, while the third was the equally dissolute Lord March, later to become the Duke of Queensberry and known in later life as 'Old Q'.

Selwyn, who died in 1791, bequeathed the girl £20,000 while Queensberry was to leave her money and property worth around £100,000 — enormous sums for that time. This meant that Mie-

Stately 'Gossip'

Mie, as the girl was known, was a prized asset in marriage even though her parentage was so doubtful. She later married Francis Charles Seymour-Conway, Lord Yarmouth, the 3rd Marchess of Hertford. Perhaps appropriately given Mie-Mie's background, he also became known as one of the most dissolute men of his generation, addicted to the good life and foreign travel.

Nocturnal Events at The Vyne

The novelist Jane Austen was a frequent visitor to The Vyne, a house dating from the sixteenth century in Hampshire, but one shudders to think what she would have made of the exploits attributed to Lord Charles Beresford there at the end of the nineteenth century. The amorous aristocrat had, he thought, made a conquest among one of the attractive guests at the house and made plans to visit her room in the dead of night. Having apparently ascertained which room was hers, he silently crept into it that very same night, stripped off his night clothes and jumped in splendid nakedness upon the bed crying 'Cock-a-doodle-doo!' to his intended paramour as he did so. At first there was a stunned silence, then the sound of someone lighting the bedside lamp – to reveal that his lordship was in bed not with his would-be lover but with a shocked Bishop of Chester and his equally startled wife.

Wisely, Lord Charles Beresford left the house the next morning before daybreak.

Stately 'Gossip'

The Snuff Fancier of Elvaston Castle

The 4th Earl of Harrington, Charles Stanhope, devoted much of his life to the pursuit of pleasure. Known during much of the Regency as Lord Petersham – he only acceded to the earldom in 1829 – Stanhope established a reputation as a dandy and a leader of fashion. More than once he took this to extremes. For a while he was infatuated with an attractive widow named Mary Browne. The phase passed but in tribute to the woman he decided to surround himself with the colour brown. Thus Lord Petersham had a brown carriage, brown horses, brown livery, brown top hats and spurs for his coachman. When he required a new coat for court he had one made in brown silk embroidered with dead leaves.

His lordship also had a passion for snuff, and reputedly had a different snuff box for each day of the year, a very dandy-like practice. One day a friend was admiring Petersham's elegant light-blue Sevres snuff box when his lordship smiled weakly and replied: 'Yes it is a nice summer box, but it would not do for winter wear.'

Unlike many dandies, however, Charles Stanhope genuinely loved women as much as himself and was often involved in intrigues and scandals. One of the worst was when he was having an affair with the gorgeous Lady Frances Webster, and her husband tried to horsewhip Petersham in the middle of the street. Later in life he again shocked society by marrying Maria Foote, a Covent Garden actress, who was seventeen years his junior. Contrary to most contemporary expectations they made a very happy couple and the Earl and Countess of Harrington held some of the best parties of their day at Harrington House in London and at their family home, Elvaston Castle near Derby. It was here that the pair had the entrance hall re-styled and called the Hall of the Fair Star, and it was dedicated to the chivalrous pursuit of love.

The Perils of Newmarket

The 4th Earl of Chesterfield was a man who knew the dangers of gambling and decided to do something about it in his own family. He made it a stipulation in his will that if his successor kept racehorses or hounds and went to the Newmarket races, or if he lost £300 or more in a day in gambling then he was immediately to forfeit £5,000 to the Dean of Westminster. The Earl actually disliked the Dean of Westminster but chose him as the beneficiary because he knew from experience that the cleric would not be slow at claiming the money.

Another member of the upper classes, Sir Thomas Coke from Norfolk, had good reason to dislike Newmarket too. He once lost so much money at the races that he had to sell the horse that had taken him there. In later years whenever Sir Thomas passed by Newmarket in his carriage he pulled down the blinds so he could not see it, and instructed his son to do the same, saying: 'Never look at the place!'

Stately 'Gossip'

The Lion of Colney Hall

ew country houses have a more unusual – and more tragic – story than that of Colney Hall in Norfolk. In the early twentieth century the impressive house was owned by the Barclay family. The Barclays had three daughters who were lively, not to say capricious ,young women who proved themselves more than a match for a series of governesses who had tried to bring order to their chaotic lives.

Now for reasons that remain unclear, the girls took it into their heads that what they really needed – or at least wanted – was a pet lion. Their conditions were quite clear; if they did not get a pet lion they would not do any work. Hard as it may be to imagine, the girls got their way and eventually a lion cub was found abroad and brought to the rather different surroundings of the Norfolk manor house (some reports even suggest the Barclay sisters had *two* lions as pets). The three sisters were delighted and looked after the cub well, though they were less kind to their little brother whom they teased mercilessly. The little boy was understandably miffed at being pushed around by his older sisters and in turn he took this out on the pet lion. The cub, which was growing in size and strength by the day, at first took the tail pulling and teasing in good part. But one day the little boy pushed the game rather too far, poked the lion once too often, and with a roar it attacked the unfortunate lad. He never recovered from his injuries.

The reaction of the three sisters perhaps sums up their attitude to life at the time. 'Silly boy,' said one of them. 'We told him not to tease it.'

The Affair of the Apricot Tart

The Regency dandy Lord Alvanley was a connoisseur of fine food, as his figure was to reflect in later life. To win a competition among his friends to see who could devise the most expensive dish, Alvanley came up with a fricassee made from the very choicest cuts of no fewer than three hundred birds. In all Alvanley used thirteen different species of bird for the culinary creation, including forty woodcock and one hundred snipe. The cost: a staggering £108 5s. Alvanley's prize was a free dinner at the famous London club White's.

The same noble gourmand also took such a fancy to an apricot tart that he asked his chef to prepare one every day for the next year, 'just in case' he wanted to eat the dish again. When his prudent steward tactfully suggested this might be a rather extravagant thing to do, Alvanley abruptly told him to go ahead and order the ingredients and added: 'Don't plague me any more about the expense.'

Stately 'Gossip'

Waddesdon Manor and the Monkeys

Guests have to be prepared for most things at country houses and stately homes. But few of those invited to a grand dinner at Waddesdon Manor can have anticipated what they found when they arrived at the table. It was near the end of the nineteenth century and the manor had not long been completed by Baron Ferdinand de Rothschild on its hilltop site near Aylesbury in Buckinghamshire. The building was and still is startling enough; it was after all built in the style of a sixteenth-century French château. Yet as the great and the good sat down for dinner they had rather more on their minds than the imposing elegance of the building. For they noticed that there were empty chairs in between each of the guests. There was much puzzlement and bemusement before all became clear. At a set signal twelve monkeys, all exquisitely dressed, made their way to the table and promptly sat down in the empty seats.

A Fitting End

The 7th Lord Newborough was a remarkable character. During the Second World War he took part in the daring raid on the French port of St Nazaire and was captured by the Germans. Imprisoned in Colditz, he managed to escape the forbidding fortress and survived to tell the tale. Later in life his lordship was accused — though he denied it — of firing a cannonball through the sail of a yacht on the Menai Straits.

Stately 'Gossip'

Even in death Lord Newborough was out of the ordinary. His last wish was to have his ashes fired out of a cannon by his son, the 8th Lord Newborough, and spread over his beloved woodland at their home in North Wales – a request that was carried out to the letter.

Lambs' Tales

Lady Melbourne, the mother of the nineteenth-century prime minister Lord Melbourne, had a relaxed view about the faithfulness between married couples. She told one young bride that her duty was to provide her husband with a male heir; once that task was complete she was free to amuse herself, said her ladyship. It was a view that Lady Melbourne certainly practised as well as she preached. She had affairs with the Duke of Bedford, Lord Coleraine and the Prince of Wales. While her eldest son was definitely her husband's, it was widely accepted that at least two of her five children were the children of another lover, Lord Egremont. One of these, William Lamb, was the man destined to become prime minister and the young Queen Victoria's friend and political mentor.

Lamb – or Lord Melbourne as he would become – also had a chequered life in matters of the heart. His wife Lady Caroline Ponsonby, whom he married in 1805, was the daughter of Lady Bessborough whom the poet Byron memorably described as being the 'hack whore of the last century'. This did not stop the same Lord

Stately 'Gossip'

Byron having an affair with Lady Caroline after her marriage, an affair that caused a huge scandal in 1812.

One peculiar aspect of Byron's affair with William Lamb's wife Caroline was that the poet was also a good friend of Lamb's mother, the afore-mentioned Lady Melbourne. Indeed Byron hinted that had Lady Melbourne been a little younger he might well have had an affair with her too. What made life even more complicated was that William and Caroline Lamb – who was barely on speaking terms with her mother-in-law – lived on one floor of Melbourne House in London while Lady Melbourne occupied another, and that there was just one entrance. As a result each woman knew when Byron was visiting the other.

Byron's affair with Lady Caroline reached a dramatic conclusion in 1813 when he snubbed her at a party and she tried to kill herself first with a broken glass and then by stabbing herself with a pair of scissors. Her more considered response to being jilted by the great man was to write an instantly best-selling novel called *Glenarvon*, in which she got her revenge by creating characters who were very obviously based on Byron and her many critics in society.

Stately 'Gossip'

There's Something in the Soup

here was mounting concern at Townend, a charming seventeenth-century home at Troutbeck in the Lake District, about the conduct of the family's butler. One could tolerate a certain amount of drinking by the staff, but on one embarrassing occasion the decanter of sherry had run out while pre-dinner drinks were being served for important guests. Someone had clearly been at the sherry, and all the evidence pointed towards the family's old soak of a butler. The problem was to know what to do about it. At a family gathering it was tentatively suggested that the butler might be taught a lesson if the sherry decanter was topped up not with more sherry, but with a similar-looking but altogether less pleasant liquid provided by one of the men of the family.

The idea seemed a little over the top, but no one came up with a better suggestion and so several males in the family were deputed to fill up the sherry decanter. The family then sat back to see whether the butler would take the hint.

A week later and the family was in a state of some anxiety. Not only had the butler appeared not to have noticed the changed nature of the decanter's contents, but the vessel was also now nearly empty. The ruse would have to be stopped, if only for the sake of the butler's health, and he must instead be tackled head on about the rapid disappearance of the sherry. So the butler was summoned to appear before his employers and was asked to account for the fact that nearly an entire decanter had been used in a week when none of the family had drunk any sherry and there had been no guests.

The butler appeared hurt at the insinuation behind the question. Surely the family recalled, he said, how they had once advised him that a couple of spoonfuls of sherry improved the flavour of soup, and that the family had been served soup almost every day that week?

The Tragedy of Squire Mytton

It was not unusual for members of the aristocracy and landed gentry to squander their inheritances, yet not many can have done it as thoroughly as the Shropshire squire, John 'Jack' Mytton.

Born in 1796, Mytton had all the advantages a person at that time could have wanted: five fine homes, including Halston Hall, a legacy of £70,000 and an annual income estimated at £10,000 a year. These were colossal sums for the time. Yet within four decades Mytton was dead, having spent all the money and accumulated huge debts, and having drunk, fought and gambled his way around his county and other parts of England.

From an early age Mytton had no sense of self-restraint or discipline. He would drink up to eight bottles of port a day – plus brandy –

owned some 1,000 hats and 3,000 shirts, drove his horse and carriages like a lunatic and once boxed twenty rounds with a miner. On one occasion Mytton rode into dinner astride a bear, which objected to the man's urgings to go faster and bit him on the leg. The squire also rode his horse indoors, hunted while naked and once lost thousands of pounds he had won gambling at the races when the wind blew the money away; he was simply quite incapable of dealing with money.

As Mytton's excesses increased along with his debts, he was forced to flee the country for Calais, where the debauchery continued. Once he suffered a severe attack of hiccups and in an attempt to stop them he set fire to his nightgown. The hiccups did stop, but he also suffered severe burns and may have died if friends had not saved him. Eventually Mytton returned to England, where he inevitably ended up in prison, massively in debt and his body crippled and bloated by his excesses. He died in prison in 1834, aged just thirty-eight.

Pass The Port

A wine expert was once invited to a stately home as a guest for the weekend. However, the family of this particular house had a mischievous streak and wanted to test out this expert's abilities. Was he as good as people said or was he, as some of them believed or hoped, simply a showman?

Stately 'Gossip'

His particular expertise lay in port, so at the end of a fine dinner the port was duly passed around the table to enable the honoured guest to show what he could do. There was an expectant hush as the connoisseur sampled the port in his usual elaborate and expert fashion. Unable to contain himself any longer, one member of the family called out, 'So what do you make of it then?'

The connoisseur sat back with a knowing smile. 'It is quite superb,' he said, pronouncing the port to be a 1947 Taylor's — a very fine vintage.

At this much of the table burst into fits of giggles, much to the bemusement of the expert, who insisted that it certainly was a 1947 Taylor's and he could have made no mistake.

A kindly soul then explained to the bemused guest the reason for the mirth; they had played a trick on him. The port in question had come not from the house's superb cellars but from a supply at the local pub that had then been transferred to the house's crystal decanters.

Understandably the connoisseur was embarrassed and felt somewhat ill-treated, and equally understandably he left the house early the next morning. To the end, however, he insisted that his judgement had been correct.

In fact, so certain had this expert been about the provenance of the port, that one member of the family decided to visit the pub to find out more about this particular sample. There he asked the landlord where the port they had recently bought from him came from. The landlord showed the young man an old wooden cask from where he had poured the port, and then went down to the cellar to point to some dusty old bottles that lay on a rack. This was where the port had come from before it was poured into the cask explained the landlord.

With a growing sense of anxiety the young man picked up one of the old bottles, wiped off the years of dust, and found himself staring at a label that read 'Taylor's 1947'. Two things were now immediately apparent: the expert had been right all along, and this fine vintage port had somehow been stolen from the stately home's cellars.

It later transpired that the family's own butler had been selling the port to local pubs. As for the wine expert, the family to their credit felt obliged to inform him of his belated triumph.

Royal Flush

Sir Thomas Beecham the great and eccentric conductor once met a distinguished-looking woman in a smart hotel and was certain he knew her, yet was equally certain he could not remember just who exactly she was. For a few moments they conversed politely, but still Sir Thomas had gained no clue as to her identity. At last he decided to ask a more direct question to see if that would do the trick. 'And your brother,' he murmured, 'is he well? What's he doing nowadays?'

'Thank you for asking, he's very well,' replied the woman. 'And he's still king.'

On the Cards

When the 1st Earl of Cadogan lost heavily at cards playing with the Duke of Richmond, the Earl saved his honour by agreeing to marry his daughter Lady Sarah to the Duke's son Lord March.

It had all the hallmarks of a disaster. Their offspring were young teenagers at the time and Lady Sarah was, in the opinion of the young Lord March, somewhat 'dowdy'. Accordingly their wedding was a fairly awkward affair, and soon afterwards the relieved young man went off on a grand tour of Europe while Lady Sarah resumed her education.

Lord March returned home a few years later, yet was not keen to renew immediate relations with his 'dowdy' young wife so went to the theatre instead. While there his gaze fell on a beautiful young woman in a box and he excitedly asked his companion who she was. He was informed that the young woman was currently the 'toast of the town'. Moreover, she was also Lady March – his wife.

Their subsequent married life was a happy one, and they had twelve children, one of whom, Lady Caroline Lennox, was the mother of the Regency politician Charles James Fox.

The Common Touch

T he attitude taken by employers to their staff reveals a great deal about their 'nobility' in its broadest sense. The Marchioness of Londonderry, one of the most intimidating society ladies of her day, once found a very junior parlour maid trying each of the chairs in her drawing-room in turn when she re-entered having said goodbye to her afternoon tea guests.

The look of horror on the poor girl's face showed that she was expecting a sound ticking off at the discovery, but her mistress summed up the situation in a flash. Edward VII had been among the company that had just departed.

'That was the chair the King sat on,' she told the maid with uncharacteristic gentleness. 'Why don't you sit down on it yourself?'

Tea with a Horse

T he Right Honourable Sir Gerald Hugh Tyrwhitt Wilson, who in 1918 succeeded to the title the 14th Lord Berners, was a man of genuine talent, a musician who wrote the score to ballets and a talented costume designer too. Berners spoke many languages, worked as a British diplomat in Constantinople (now Istanbul) and was a friend to the powerful and famous of his day. He was also decidedly eccentric. Berners painted his doves in bright colours, had a harpsichord installed in his Rolls-Royce so he could play the instrument as he was chauffered around the country and held wild and unpredictable parties at his home at Faringdon House in Berkshire.

Once he invited a ballet dancer, Robert Helpmann, to take tea with him at Faringdon. The dancer was astonished to find that as he took tea in the drawing room Lord Berners was feeding hot buttered scones to another guest – a horse. Eventually the horse had eaten its fill and was gently led out of the room. Later Berners explained why the horse had been there. He said that he was usually nervous when meeting people, and so the horse was present to make the guests equally nervous. This helped his lordship to overcome his own nerves and then everyone could settle down for a 'normal' conversation.

Dressed for Dinner

The Earl of Bridgewater Francis Henry Egerton was a scholar and collector of books, as well as being one of the more oddly behaved members of the British aristocracy. He had a passion for animals, and used to give dinner parties to which dogs were invited. Moreover, they were also dressed for dinner, right down to special shoes their master had made for them. The Earl clearly had a thing about shoes, for he used to wear a different pair each day and then arrange them in rows. By examining the worn sole on each pair he could thus chart the passing of time.

Though an animal lover, Bridgewater was also a keen shot, and continued to carry on shooting even in old age. As his eyesight failed he had the wings of pigeons and partridges in his grounds clipped, so that he could still shoot them. Perhaps it was unsurprising that Egerton was the 8th and final Earl of Bridgewater; after all he was clearly far too busy being eccentric ever to have got married and produce an heir.

Squire of All England

George Osbaldeston, born in 1786, was a famous sportsman of his day who became known by many as the 'Squire of All England' because of his many exploits. Curiously for such a vigorous man he chose to buy and live in Ebberston Hall in North Yorkshire, an attractive but tiny eighteenth-century Palladian mansion once described as the smallest stately home in England.

Osbaldeston was a famed horseman and once won a 1,000-guinea bet that he could ride two hundred miles in under ten hours, using an unlimited supply of horses. In fact dressed in a 'purple silk jacket, black velvet cap, doeskin breeches, and top boots' the Squire managed the feat in under nine hours, using a four-mile long course at Newmarket. The sportsman was also a very good shot, and it was said he could shoot a flying pigeon with the (notoriously inaccurate) pistols of his day.

Osbaldeston once fought a famous duel with Lord George Bentinck over a gambling debt, but thanks to the astuteness of Lord Bentinck's second, Colonel Anson, who counted down to the signal to fire in such a way that he confused Osbaldeston, the Squire's shot for once missed his target and honour was satisfied.

The gallant Squire was also wont to use his sporting ability to show off to women, and once rode more than twenty miles to find an orchid to impress a woman whom he admired. Alas, Osbaldeston's life ended in relative poverty, and in his later years he was reduced to bartering his home's furniture for drink.

The Inventor of Gnomes

ir Charles Isham, 10th Baronet, who lived at the family home at Lamport Hall in Northamptonshire, was a fascinating character. A keen gardener, he travelled widely to pick up new ideas with which to improve his fine garden. During a trip to Nuremberg in the 1840s Sir Charles was fascinated by some tiny little terracotta figures he saw and later had twenty-one of them imported to his estate. Here he set them among the boulders in his large rock garden armed with picks and shovels as if they were mining the area. Some of them were even given little banners that read 'On strike'.

Stately 'Gossip'

These charming little figures were of course the first garden gnomes to have been brought to Britain. However, then just as now, they were not to everyone's taste. Sir Charles' daughters hated the little gnomes and later had them all removed, apart from one who was hidden in a crevice in the garden. This little chap – nicknamed 'Lampy' – has survived as the oldest gnome in the country and in the 1990s was insured for £1 million.

The Noble Miser

Sir Harvey Elwes was an extremely mean and extremely rich man who lived in the eighteenth century. His vast fortune – some £250,000 – went to his nephew John who set about becoming even meaner and wealthier than his uncle had been. To this end Elwes rode his horses on grass to avoid wearing out their shoes, used all back routes to avoid toll roads, retired to bed when night fell to avoid paying for lighting, travelled with a hard-boiled egg about his person to avoid having to buy lunch and rarely if ever saw a doctor – because of the cost. On one occasion when he had a problem with his legs Elwes felt obliged, very reluctantly, to seek medical advice. Yet even now he still managed to avoid paying. For Elwes cunningly made a wager with the doctor, as a result of which the medic treated one leg and left the other unattended. If both legs healed at the same rate then the doctor had agreed to forfeit his fee. Sure enough both legs got better at the same rate and the old miser was spared paying his medical bill.

All this meant that when he died in 1789, Elwes had amassed a mighty fortune of more than £700,000, even if he had endured a pretty miserable life to achieve such wealth.

All's Well

The 1st Baron Alvanley, Richard Arden (sometimes also spelled Arderne), was a friend of William Pitt, brilliant lawyer and a politician. His son William, the 2nd Baron, was alas an altogether less substantial character, whose activities both as a soldier and a society 'buck' — he was a friend of the Prince Regent — eventually frittered away the family fortune and lands. Among his expensive tastes he included a fondness for visiting brothels from an early age.

Even getting involved in duels seemed to cost Lord Alvanley money. The Irish political leader, Daniel O'Connell, once publicly referred to Alvanley as a 'bloated buffoon', which was admittedly an accurate reflection of his lordship's girth at the time. However, this was an insult that Alvanley was obliged to respond to and so he challenged O'Connell to a duel. The latter refused, as he had already killed a man once in a contest. Alvanley may have been secretly pleased but to save face he then had to threaten the Irishman with a horsewhipping. As a result, and to save his father from this humiliation, O'Connell's son decided to fight the duel on his father's behalf.

Stately 'Gossip'

After the duel on Wimbledon Common had ended with shots fired but no death or injury on either side, a relieved Arden returned to his coachman and drove home. As they pulled up at Alvanley's house the peer surprised the coachman by giving him a whole sovereign for his efforts. 'It's a great deal for only having taken your lordship to Wimbledon!' he protested.

Alvanley managed a thin smile as he insisted the coachman took the money. 'My good man, I give it you not for taking me,' he said, 'but for bringing me back.'

The Silent Treatment

Lady Asquith, wife of the British prime minister Herbert Asquith, and better known as Margot, was one of the most forthright and fascinating personalities of her day. Never backwards in coming forward, and having a rather high opinion of herself, she delighted and irritated her contemporaries in equal measure. Reviewing Margot's autobiography in 1922, the acerbic Dorothy Parker said the affair between Margot Asquith and Margot Asquith was one of the 'prettiest love stories' in literature.

Meanwhile another (future) British prime minister Arthur Balfour was once asked if the rumours that he and Margot Tennant (as she then was) were going to get married were true. Balfour paused briefly and said, 'No, I rather think of having a career of my own.'

Stately 'Gossip'

Margot famously had a wicked tongue of her own. She had a poor view of the ability of Lord Kitchener, who was in charge of the British military in the First World War, remarking that he was 'not a great man, but at least he was a great poster'.

She also had a famous encounter with the platinum blonde film star Jean Harlow. The actress went up to Lady Asquith and said, 'Are you Margot Asquith?' mispronouncing her Christian name.

'My dear, the "t" is silent,' retorted Lady Asquith, 'as in Harlow.'

A Final Experiment

The 1st Baron Verulam, Francis Bacon, was Lord Chancellor of England and also a scientist who believed in the power of experiments to prove scientific theory, rather than just relying on reasoning. Sadly this noble interest in experiments led to his demise. In 1626 he was driving through snowy streets in north London in his carriage when it suddenly occurred to him that snow might be used as a means of keeping food cool and thus preserving it. So he stopped the coach, went and bought a chicken at a woman's house, killed it and then stuffed it full of snow. The experiment did indeed suggest that food could be kept longer in this way, but unfortunately Bacon, who was in his sixties, had got very cold during the exercise and developed pneumonia. He died three days later.

Stately 'Gossip'

The Fatness of Prince George

George Bryan Brummell came from relatively obscure middle class origins to become for a time one of the most influential if ultimately vacuous figures in Regency society. Known as 'Beau' Brummell, he was a dandy and leader of fashion, as well as being considered a wit. Much of his influence stemmed from his friendship with the Prince Regent – later George IV. Accordingly Brummell's star began to wane after a falling out with the prince, a split that was to cause much excitement in society.

The *froideur* on the prince's side was shown at a ball in 1814 when the future king came across Brummell and his friend and fellow dandy Lord Alvanley. The prince acknowledged Alvanley, whom he also knew well, but completely ignored Brummell. The spurned dandy was usually noted for his self-control but on this occasion he 'lost it'. For Brummell turned to his companion and said in a loud stage whisper for all to hear: 'Who's your fat friend?'

The prince, who was notoriously vain about his appearance, never forgave his former friend for this remark and Brummell's already weakened position in society was doomed. As so many dandies did, Brummell had lived way beyond his means and to escape his debts was later forced to flee to France where he died penniless and insane in 1840.

Stately 'Gossip'

Wartime Gaffe

American heiress Maud Burke became Lady Cunard after marrying the British baronet Sir Bache Cunard; her daughter was the author Nancy Cunard. Before that she had been best known for having a tempestuous affair with the then popular American writer George Moore. She was not perhaps noted for her high intellect and political acumen. At a great ball in London shortly after the end of the Second World War, a fellow guest pointed to the splendour and glitz of the members of society enjoying themselves in front of them and remarked, '*This* is what we fought the war for.'

Pausing only briefly Lady Cunard replied, 'Oh, do you mean they are all Poles?'

The Cricketing Lord

Lord Frederic Beauclerk, who was reputed to have been a direct descendant of King Charles II and his famous mistress Nell Gwynne, was by profession the vicar of St Albans in Hertfordshire. But this occupation seems to have taken a back seat to the chief passion in his life – cricket. This he combined with another absorbing interest – making money – by betting on cricket matches, usually those in which he played and thus whose outcome he could influence.

Stately 'Gossip'

In the first half of the nineteenth century, and after his playing days were over, he used to boast that he made the considerable sum of 600 guineas a year from gambling on cricket matches. None of this stopped him becoming the second president of the MCC — Marylebone Cricket Club — a prestigious organisation that became the driving force of English cricket. Given His Lordship's propensity for gambling on games, this was perhaps surprising.

Beauclerk — described by one observer as an 'unmitigated scoundrel' — took part in a notoriously 'bent' cricket match played in 1817 between England and Nottingham. It appears both teams had promised to lose the match — for betting purposes — and there ensued a farcical match in which each team tried to surrender wickets and give away runs. Ironically Beauclerk was not in on this betting scam and was apparently furious at events, partly because he broke a finger trying to stop a deliberate overthrow by a team-mate. As a result Beauclerk, who was himself a gifted amateur player, decided to ruin the career of a team mate, a professional by the name of William Lambert. Beauclerk produced evidence to the MCC that Lambert had 'not tried' during the notorious England/Nottingham match and the player was effectively banned from competitive cricket for life.

Another of Beauclerk's passions was horses and horse racing and he used to ride at Epsom under various aliases so that his bishop would not find out what he was doing. The vicar even had the seat of his own pulpit made in the shape of a saddle.

Stately 'Gossip'

A Stroll After Supper

Viscount Haldane of Cloan, who was twice Lord Chancellor of Britain and helped found the London School of Economics, was a man who liked his food and accordingly acquired a considerable girth. One night at dinner with fellow peers in London, Haldane – born Richard Burdon – was ribbed about his size. Haldane, who died in 1928, acknowledged his ample proportions, but rationally pointed out to the gathered company – he was after all a noted philosopher as well as lawyer – that just because he was quite fat this did not necessarily mean he was unfit. Indeed to prove this Lord Haldane vowed he would walk the sixty miles to Brighton right there and then, wearing his current evening clothes, and would take no more than two minutes rest in each hour until he reached his destination. Once in Brighton he would send a telegram informing his friends that he had made it. And Haldane was as good as his word.

An Ancient Monument

The poet Dame Edith Sitwell grew up at Renishaw Hall near Sheffield, which had been in the Sitwell family for many years. One day at lunch a rather foolish young man, who was sitting next to Edith, asked her whether she remembered the house being built. Before she could reply another guest, Alice Keppel, who had heard the question, intervened to say, 'Be careful young man! Not even the nicest girl in the world likes to be asked if she is four hundred years old.'

Stately 'Gossip'

Jumpers

he dressmaker Norman Hartnell, who designed the Coronation dress for Queen Elizabeth II, and who was knighted for his services to dressmaking and in particular to the Royal Family, was a popular figure at country house gatherings. He was once at a house when he noticed a fine silver trophy put on display by the mistress of the house. When the conversation flagged he decided to compliment his hostess on it. 'That's very kind of you,' she replied. 'I won it for one of my jumpers.'

'How clever,' replied the famed couturier. 'Would you knit one for me?'

She had of course been referring to her horses.

The Rebuilding of Constable Burton

ometimes in life our words come back to haunt us, but few can have been so damaged by seemingly innocent words as the eighteenth-century gentleman Sir Marmaduke Wyvill.

The Wyvill's family seat was at Constable Burton in Wensleydale, Yorkshire, a fine sixteenth-century house that had been the centre of Wyvill life for two centuries. It was this impressive building that Sir Marmaduke inherited in the 1760s. However, the new lord of the manor wanted to make his mark on the family home and decided to engage a local architect – one John Carr from York – to begin work on the place. So it was that one day Sir Marmaduke set off for an extended five-month tour of Scotland, leaving Carr, who was already building a considerable reputation for his designs, in charge of the work. His final instructions to the architect appear straightforward enough, if a little vague; 'Improve my residence,' Sir Marmaduke exhorted.

When, after his invigorating tour of Scotland, Sir Marmaduke returned, he did not find the glorious sixteenth-century home at Constable Burton 'improved'. In fact, Sir Marmaduke did not find the home at all. It had vanished completely. Not a single wall, room or ceiling remained.

It turned out, as an apoplectic Sir Marmaduke discovered, that John Carr had sent an advance party from York to begin the planned improvements while the architect was to follow on later to supervise the main work. Alas, somehow, and inexplicably, the first wave of workmen had managed to misconstrue the instructions and instead of beginning a modernisation had simply pulled the old structure down completely.

Remarkably, instead of having Carr made bankrupt, made to flee abroad, imprisoned or otherwise harmed, the forgiving Sir Marmaduke calmed down and commissioned the architect to design and build an entirely new house in 1768. At least this story has a happy ending. For though Sir Marmaduke had to find the massive sum in those days of £10,000 for the new house, the result of Carr's labours remain to this day, a magnificent classical house of dressed stone.

This impressive house helped make Carr's reputation, too. In fact the architectural expert and art historian Nikolaus Pevsner praised the structure as a 'very perfect mid-Georgian house, a square of beautiful ashlar stone with nothing sticking out'.

So after his distinctly unpromising start at Constable Burton John Carr went on to earn a considerable fortune as an architect and eventually became Lord Mayor of York.

Meanwhile Sir Marmaduke, who at least had a fine new house for his troubles, was more careful over his choice of words after that.

The Duke and his Toothbrush

I f one is used to living in the luxurious surroundings of a home such as Blenheim Palace, then perhaps one can be forgiven for feeling somewhat disoriented by life when staying elsewhere. One day the 10th Duke of Marlborough was staying at the home of one of his three daughters. In the morning she was surprised to hear her father upstairs complaining loudly about the fact that his toothbrush was 'not working'. It transpired that the Duke's toothbrush was not producing the foam that he was used to, and he wanted another. It had to be gently explained to John Spencer-Churchill that to produce foam on a toothbrush one first had to add toothpaste. Apparently the Duke was accustomed to having this done for him at Blenheim by a valet.

The Falling Footman

Thomas Herbert, the 8th Earl of Pembroke, who became First Lord of the Admiralty and was later Lord Lieutenant of Ireland, could be an unforgiving man and was notably intolerant of servants who drank too much at the ancestral home, Wilton House in Wiltshire.

However the Earl, who was born in 1656, had something of a soft spot for one old faithful retainer called John who was employed at the house as a footman. John could get away with the odd tipple here and there and the Earl pretended not to notice. One day, though, Herbert had to take note when John appeared before him and other members of the household in such a state of intoxication that he could barely stand. Turning a blind eye was clearly not an option. Instead the Earl grabbed the footman by the arm, made a show of taking his pulse and declared: 'He is in a raging fever! Get him to bed and send for the apothecary!'

Stately 'Gossip'

The instructions were followed and for several days John the footman had to endure hideous doses of unpleasant medicine and regular bleeding, as was the custom of his time. A few days later, and restored to 'health', a pale and haggard looking footman was presented to the Earl. 'I am glad to see you alive,' said Pembroke. 'You have had a lucky escape — had I not passed by at that time and spied what condition you were in you would have been dead by now.'

The Earl paused and then added firmly, 'But John, no more of these fevers!'

Passing Fancy

William Douglas the 4th Duke of Queensberry was a friend of the Prince Regent and a notorious rogue. He never married and preferred instead to pursue a series of 'romances' with attractive young women, many of them operatic performers. For years he used to bathe in milk, supposedly to maintain his 'potency'. In his later years Queensberry, known as 'Old Q', was too old to do much active philandering or chasing of women, and instead spent many hours each day in the window of his home in Piccadilly admiring the attractions of passing young women.

He still needed servants, of course, and one day was reviewing young men for the post of 'running footman', whose job entailed running errands, taking messages and clearing a way through crowds for his master. Old Q insisted that as a test applicants should dress up in the household's fine and expensive uniform and then run up and down Piccadilly to show their mettle. On this occasion a bright fit young man donned the expensive clothes and sped up and down the busy streets. An impressed Old Q shouted out from his window: 'You'll do very well for me!' To which the rapidly disappearing young man cheekily responded: 'And your lordship's fine livery will do very well for me too.' He was never seen again.

Unwelcome Guests

ome hosts and hostesses of stately homes are more tactful than others when it comes to dealing with guests who have overstayed their welcome. Lady Ela Russell, mistress of Chorleywood House near Rickmansworth, used to walk around the house saying in a loud stage whisper: 'I wish they'd go! I wish they'd go!' By all accounts they usually did – and quickly.

Staged Fright

otley Abbey, which dates from the twelfth century and where the great warrior king Henry V once stayed, was appropriately enough owned by Laurence Olivier and Vivien Leigh. Olivier was of course famous for his portrayal of the king in Shakespeare's *Henry V*.

Stately 'Gossip'

From time to time acting colleagues of the couple visited the Buckinghamshire abbey. On one occasion the guests were Ralph Richardson and his wife. Richardson had had a bad experience of visiting Olivier and Vivien Leigh's home in London, where he accidentally set light to some curtains and ornate cornicing with a firework. So naturally the actor was determined to be extra careful this time, lest he once more incur the wrath of the volatile Vivien Leigh. After a pleasant dinner, during which the usual theatrical stories were trotted out, Olivier asked if anyone wanted to see the paintings left behind on some of the roof beams by the earlier occupants, the monks. Richardson was keen to have a look and so the pair of great actors went up to the attic to examine the medieval paintings close up.

Before long, however, the rest of the household was startled by a loud crash and then a cry. They rushed upstairs to find Ralph Richardson lying uninjured but thoroughly miserable on a bed in a guestroom, gazing up at a gaping hole in the ceiling above him. The great actor had got so carried away with the old paintings he had put his foot on the unprotected lath and plaster and had fallen straight through it.

Intimidated by Goodwood

uring the Second World War an American couple in Washington became friends with a British couple who were living next door. The Americans got on so well with their friends

Stately 'Gossip'

Freddie and Betty Richmond that they accepted an invitation to visit them in the UK after the war. A few years later, and with the war over, the couple from Washington arrived in Europe and made contact with their British friends who in turn were delighted to hear from them and repeated their invitation to come and stay.

The arrangements were made and it was agreed that Freddie would meet the pair off the train and drive them to his home. The reunion took place at the railway station and all was proceeding well until the car neared Freddie's home. The Americans were overwhelmed to see that Freddie and Betty did not live in a house but what was to them a palace. In fact what the American couple had not apparently appreciated was that 'Freddie Richmond' was the 9th Duke of Richmond, 'Betty' was Elizabeth, Duchess of Richmond, and that their family home was the utterly magnificent Goodwood House in West Sussex.

Sadly the American pair were so intimidated by the house and servants – and by the way the butler swiftly unpacked all their clothes in their wonderful room – that they fled the place as soon as they could. It was all rather puzzling to 'Freddie and Betty' who were by common consent about as down to earth and unstuffy aristocrats as one could wish to find.

Stately 'Gossip'

The Dancing Sandwich

he 4th Earl of Sandwich, John Montagu, was a controversial figure in his lifetime, even if down the centuries he is best known for lending his name to a snack contained between two pieces of bread. (The story was that the Earl, a keen gambler, ate his food in this way so he did not have to leave the gaming table.)

He proved unpopular for his part in the prosecution of journalist and politician John Wilkes; Sandwich had previously been a friend of Wilkes and public opinion disapproved of the Earl's change of allegiance. The Earl also had the misfortune to be in charge of the British navy at a less than distinguished time in its history, the 1770s.

He seems to have had a remarkable gift for upsetting people more personally too. The Earl once deeply offended his chaplain by dressing up a baboon in clerical clothes so that it could 'say' grace before dinner. Then, when staying in France, Sandwich, who was noted for his untidy not to say clumsy way of moving and even walking, chose to have dancing lessons from a Parisian teacher. After the lessons were complete and as he was about to depart back to Britain the Earl, doubtless trying to be helpful, thanked the teacher for his help and suggested that he would recommend the maestro to his society friends in London.

The dance teacher looked horrified, then said to the Earl calmly but fervently: 'I would regard it as a particular favour if your lordship would *never* tell anyone from whom you learned to dance.'

Shaw's Corner

The great playwright George Bernard Shaw decided to buy a house in an English village because he had been told that people there lived to a fine old age. The property he chose in 1906 was 'The Villa' in Ayot St Lawrence in Hertfordshire, though he quickly renamed it with characteristic modesty 'Shaw's Corner'. The Edwardian villa, which is now run by the National Trust, seems to have worked, because when Shaw died in 1943 he had reached the impressive age of ninety-four.

Never Ending Story

The ageing 4th Duke of Queensberry had many fine houses, including one in Piccadilly and another on Richmond Hill, overlooking the Thames with what is still regarded as one of the best views in southern England. The irascible old duke however grew tired of visitor after visitor complimenting him on this excellent view of the river. 'I am quite tired of it,' he once exclaimed to yet another admiring guest. 'Flow, flow flow, always the same!'

Stately 'Gossip'

Wiping Out the Past

One has to feel a certain sympathy for Baronet Sir Ian Grantley, despite the fact that he was a landowner on an epic scale in Northumberland in the nineteenth century. Indeed, so vast were his estates that Sir Ian, though by no means a stupid man, could not always recall all his homes and buildings. So one day when he came across the name Fortescue Castle, the Baronet felt a faint sentiment that he somehow knew it. As well as the distant recollection, however, there was also a tinge of dread, like that feeling you have when awakening from a terrible hangover, convinced that you have done something awful the night before but cannot remember what. It was therefore with some trepidation that he asked his wife whether she too had any recollection of the place.

Lady Grantley was surprised and understandably a little hurt at the question; after all, that was where the couple had spent a few days immediately after their honeymoon. In that case, persisted Sir Ian, with the feeling of dread growing ever stronger, who owned Fortescue Castle? On being told that it was the Baronet himself who owned the building the dreadful feeling turned to near certainty. He immediately ordered a carriage and he and his bewildered wife swiftly made the journey across country to the mysterious Fortescue Castle. When they arrived at the scene it was just as Sir Ian feared. There was no longer a Fortescue Castle.

Only now did the full story come flooding back into his mind. So bad was his experience during those days spent at Fortescue with his new bride that he had told one of his agents not — as others might have done — to sell the castle but to have the entire structure torn down.

History does not record exactly what explanation Sir Ian gave to his wife, but it must have been an interesting journey back home.

The Mini Duke

The late 11th Duke of Northumberland once entered the yard at his family home at Syon House in south-west London when a member of staff approached him in some anxiety.

'Your Grace,' said the maintenance man, 'somebody must have dumped this load of old junk here last night.' At this the staff member pointed to a tatty old Mini car parked in a corner of the yard, a vehicle that had clearly seen better days. 'I'll call the scrap man and have it taken away immediately,' he added.

The Duke smiled and informed his loyal employee that would not be necessary. 'The car is mine and I'm going to use it in London,' he told the astonished employee. 'It should stop me being recognised so often.'

Stately 'Gossip'

The Bishop of Ickworth

Ickworth House in Suffolk is one of the more remarkable buildings in Britain, an extraordinary structure with a large central rotunda and curved corridors. The unusual features of this National Trust structure are perhaps appropriate, for its creator was an equally remarkable and extraordinary character called Frederick Augustus Hervey, otherwise known as the Bishop of Derry and the 4th Earl of Bristol. Indeed, one of the unusual facts about Hervey is that though he started work on Ickworth in 1795, he never lived inside the house nor indeed did he ever return to see it. For Hervey was a born traveller and collector, and he spent the last years of his life – he died in 1803 – travelling across Continental Europe in search of ever more treasures to send back to his new 'home' at Ickworth.

Hervey cut an unusual figure for a bishop, even by the standards of the eighteenth century. According to one observer the Bishop was 'a bad father, a worse husband…very blasphemous in his conversation and greatly addicted to intrigue and gallantry.'

Among other dalliances, Hervey had a notorious and scandalous affair with the Countess Lichtenau, who was the ambitious mistress of Frederick William II of Prussia. However his libidinous nature did not stop him from taking a disapproving interest in the love lives of others. At his home at Downhill, Coleraine, in Northern Ireland, Hervey discreetly sprinkled flour on the carpets in the hope that he could tell who was visiting whom at night among the guests and servants. The flamboyantly dressed Earl also had a healthy appetite for food, and when on the move he would dispatch his own cook to the next inn, so that a suitably lavish feast would await his weary entourage when they arrived.

Though a cultured and refined man, Hervey also seems to have had something of a temper. During a trip to Italy, the good Bishop apparently took exception to the incessant tinkling of bells by members of a Corpus Christi procession, and in his rage threw a tureen of soup at the passing troop. Because of this misdemeanour the papal authorities forced him to leave the area.

The Earl also fell foul of another key power in continental Europe at the time – Napoleon. The French military genius took exception to Hervey's plundering of Italy's finest works of art simply to decorate his own home, and had the Earl imprisoned at Milan for eighteen months. The Bishop later resumed his travels but his health, which had never been robust and had forced him to seek out some of Europe's finest health resorts, began to fade fast. He died at Albano in Italy in July 1803, apparently in the outbuilding of an Italian peasant – it seems the poor Catholic could not bring himself to allow a Protestant cleric into his home.

Hervey's last words were said to have been 'Ickworth, the house ....' The great building, which was already under construction by this time, had remained an obsession of this remarkable man to the end. And though he never saw it in life, he came close to it in death – his body was taken back to England and buried at Ickworth church.

An Inside Job

The Wolseleys are an old, traditional and much respected county family who lived for centuries at Wolseley Hall in Staffordshire (the hall was demolished in 1967). Yet this did not stop Sir Charles Wolseley, 7th Baronet, from indulging in some radical politics in his day. His revolutionary zeal was fired by his experiences as a young man while he was travelling through France in 1789. The young baronet became caught up in events leading to the French Revolution and even took part in the storming of the Bastille on 14 July. Back in England, where much of society feared a similar upheaval, Sir Charles' views did not go down well. He was imprisoned for inciting riot, though he could have escaped jail had he issued a public apology – this he refused. Instead he spent eighteen months in jail, an experience he claimed to have enjoyed. Perhaps this can be explained by the laxness of his incarceration and the fact that he seemed to have rather more access to the outside world than many current prisoners enjoy. For during his time in prison Sir Charles had plenty of time to arrange the modernisation of Wolseley Hall, even if history and the bulldozers suggest this project was not a complete triumph. Moreover, it appears that Sir Charles' youngest son was born two weeks before he was released...

Stately 'Gossip'

Not Cricket

The late cricket commentator and veteran broadcaster Brian Johnston was at Eton with the Hon William Douglas-Home, son of the 13th Earl of Home and brother of Sir Alec Douglas-Home, who later became prime minister. Accordingly he became friends with the Douglas-Home family.

While still a young man Johnston once went to an hotel in London where William was staying, in order to take him to watch a Test match at Lord's cricket ground. When he arrived his old school friend informed him that his mother, Lady Home, was also staying in the hotel. Johnston naturally knew Lady Home and wanted to pay his respects to her, so asked William for the number of her room. Johnston got to the door, knocked loudly, and heard Lady Home say 'Come in!' So the young man opened the door, went into the room and to his horror found Lady Home stark naked in front of the dressing table. 'How dare you Brian!' said Lady Home at this unwelcome intrusion.

'But you said to come in,' stammered an embarrassed Johnston.

'I know,' agreed Lady Home, 'but I thought you were a waiter.'

Stately 'Gossip'

A Fond Farewell

One can picture the scene. It was just after the outbreak of war in 1914, and there was still a general air of excitement in Britain and a passionate desire by young men to do the right thing and sign up for military action. This was the view of young Archibald Dyson, scion of the Dyson family who had lived at Tyrell Hall in Gloucestershire for many generations. He volunteered and was accepted for service as a sub-lieutenant in the family's customary cavalry regiment, the 17th Lancers. At last the day arrived for Archibald to leave the bosom of his family home and to make his way to serve with his regiment at the front. The whole household lined up to say farewell at this grand but obviously moving moment. The servants were dressed in their finest, while Archibald was dressed in his best uniform and handing out gifts to those he was leaving behind. Then Archibald's father stepped forward with the family sword, thrust it into his son's scabbard and bade him to 'do his duty'. It was a fine and powerful moment. With that the young man leapt up on his horse, urged his mount forward... and then nothing. Quite unable or unwilling to rise to the occasion, Archibald's mount decided not to budge an inch but instead, to make matters even worse, to lie down quietly where it was. Fortunately the entire family, including Archibald, saw the funny side of this and everyone laughed at the anti-climax of the scene. So it was that Archibald went off to join his famous cavalry regiment in the family's old faithful pony and trap.

Curiously, the Dyson family had a particular connection with horses and war. An ancestor, Sir Charles Dyson, was on hand to give Charles Stuart his steed when the future king's own horse was killed beneath him at the Battle of Worcester in 1651. Sir Charles reportedly cried at the time, 'To the king my horse, to the enemy my life, to God my soul.' They were indeed a noble lot, the Dysons. Sir Charles' brother Hugh rode into the same battle with his sword still firmly in his scabbard rather than take the life of a fellow Englishman.

Hunting for Footmen

It was the 1950s and the Duke and Duchess of Marlborough were on their annual visit to the fine estate at Glenfiddich for the shooting season. That day the Duchess was out shooting without the Duke – they were not particularly close at the time – and she was accompanied by her young son Charles who had just been given his first gun. The Duchess, formerly Alexandra Mary Cadogan, the daughter of Viscount Chelsea, was herself a good shot and was explaining to her son the paramount importance of safety on a shoot. Above all one had to take special care never to shoot in the direction of the beaters. However, minutes later, when the grouse were starting to fly, the Duchess herself got momentarily carried away and inevitably blasted in the direction of the beaters; so close in fact that she managed to 'wing' one of the unfortunate servants who was on beating duty. As good luck would have it, he had been far enough away from the Duchess's gun for his wounds to be slight and he quickly made a full recovery.

That did not stop the Duke milking the moment for all it was worth at dinner later that evening, however. At a suitable moment of silence he turned to the Duchess and said: 'I hear you've had a good day's shooting. Eighteen grouse, five hares, fourteen rabbits – and an Italian footman.'

The Wolf of Weston Park

Orlando Bridgeman, 5th Earl of Bradford and master of Weston Park, once employed a butler by the name of Wolf. His work seemed exemplary until an embarrassing incident one day at a lunch party. Wolf had been pouring out the white wine to the guests when one of them took a sip. 'Extraordinary,' exclaimed the guest. 'This wine tastes just like cider!' His observation was backed up by several other guests who had also noticed an unusual flavour and bouquet, not to mention colour, to the 'wine'.

Naturally embarrassed by this episode – no host wants to be accused of serving cider masquerading as wine, never mind a nobleman of unimpeachable integrity – the 5th Earl decided to investigate the matter. It seems that the trusty Wolf had a dark side after all; and that the faithful butler had been drinking the cellar's fine white wines and topping up the tell-tale empties with cider. By mistake he had served the guests this very ordinary cider at luncheon and was now forced to pay the price. Though he was not charged for the wine, he left the household with no notice pay, it being deemed that he had already drunk it.

Dressing Down

he great British poet Alfred Tennyson — himself the 1st Baron Tennyson — once invited for dinner the Duke of Argyll and his family who were holidaying nearby. When the Duke and his entourage arrived at Tennyson's house the poet immediately apologised for not having changed into traditional evening attire. 'I never dress for anyone,' explained Tennyson. 'If I made an exception and dressed for a duke my butler would set me down as a snob.'

Mad Madge

argaret Lucas, who was later to become the Duchess of Newcastle, was a well-known character in the seventeenth century. Unusually for a woman at the time she was a prolific writer, and even more unusually for a duchess she published works on a range of subjects under her own name. Her eccentric behaviour and outlandish dress won her the name 'Mad Madge', though as a child she had been very shy. Madge took a close interest in science and held a few typically eccentric views of her own on the subject of nature. She believed that all winds ultimately came from the same place in the north, from Lapland, and that snow was nothing more than 'curdled' water.

Moor Disasters

he grouse moors of the north of England and Scotland are a major attraction for sportsmen from all around the world, eager to try for themselves this quintessentially British shooting environment. This draw is especially strong for Frenchmen, who are renowned for their love of shooting, even if this passion can sometimes lead them to get carried away. So it was that a French sportsman took part in a shoot one August on a grouse moor owned by a famous stately home. All was set fair for a fine day's shooting. The weather was good and there were plenty of grouse around, even if one or two of the shots, including the Frenchman, had not been on such a shoot before. All the men were lined up in a row in their shooting position, with the host taking his place at the bottom of the line where he could keep a watchful eye on most of the other shots, though a couple, including the Frenchman, were just out of sight over the brow of a hill. Once the beaters — who drive the birds up into the air — were ready the shooting began, and soon all the guns were blazing. A flock of sheep were also disturbed by the commotion, but the host happily noted that they were heading out of sight over the hill, away from danger.

Stately 'Gossip'

After a few minutes the host was starting to compliment himself on the start of a good day's shooting when he suddenly saw a local farmer come rushing over the hillside. It was an unusual sight because the local farmers usually and understandably kept well out of the way on such occasions. The host watched puzzled as the farmer waved his arms in obvious agitation, while his shouted words floated across the warm August air. 'Someone stop that maniac!' came the cry. The farmer vanished from sight, and then the host was suddenly aware that all the other men had stopped shooting and were staring in the direction of the far end of the shooting line. Sensing trouble, the host ran as fast as he could towards the end of the line and dashed over the hill, where he was greeted by a macabre sight. There was the grinning Frenchman looking very pleased with himself, surrounded by a number of very dead sheep that he had just shot. 'It is magnificent sport!' exclaimed the Frenchman in his native tongue. 'These wild sheep are fantastic!'

Nearby the farmer had momentarily turned from violent anger to deep despair and shook his head in disbelief. 'He's shot my best ram!' he stuttered in his broad local accent.

Meanwhile the Frenchman, who had failed to pick up the nuances of the local accent or indeed the body language of the farmer, and who believed the rapidly increasing group of spectators had come to praise his shooting, assumed a modest air and airily waved his hand in the air. 'Really,' he said to the onlookers, 'it's nothing, nothing at all.'

Stately 'Gossip'

Wrong Footed

One must always keep one's wits about one at dinner parties in stately homes, for all may not always be what it seems. That was the bitter lesson learnt by one British politician at a dinner at the impressive Berrington Hall in the 1960s. Berrington, which is near Leominster in Herefordshire and which has stunning views of the Brecon Beacons, was designed in the eighteenth century by Henry Holland — later architect to the Prince Regent — and among the many fine objects of interest are four large Aubusson tapestries. These tapestries were causing some excitement to a pale young man who was at the dinner party, and who was expanding elaborately on their significance to the politician who was sat opposite. However, our politician had other thoughts on his mind, notably the rather attractive and well-developed form of an ambassador's wife who was also seated across from him, next to the artistically-inclined youth.

The statesman was very impressed with the woman's charms, and so was delighted, if a little shocked, when he felt the unmistakeable touch of a delicate foot reaching under the table to his leg. Slowly the foot advanced up his leg towards his thigh and above, and the politician was by now thoroughly enjoying himself. He returned the favour by stroking and caressing the foot, all the time giving knowing smiles and looks to the ambassador's wife who in the circumstances was maintaining an impressive poise. Eventually the women at the table took their leave, and regretfully the politician bade his delightful dinner companion good evening.

There was just one small problem. Though the wife of the ambassador had left, 'her' foot remained. The reason was soon horribly obvious. The foot in question belonged to the young tapestry expert who had been sitting next to her.

Ducal Debt

Georgiana, the 5th Duke of Devonshire, was an inveterate gambler, and like most prolific gamblers, ended up massively in debt for much of her life. After her death in 1806 her son, the future 6th Duke, 'inherited' her gambling debts of around £100,000. This was despite the fact that her husband the 5th Duke had constantly paid off her betting debts during her lifetime. Not that the 6th Duke could plead poverty; from his enormous estates alone he had an annual income of some £100,000. Yet the Duke still managed to live beyond his means – spending some £17,000 more a year than he earned – and at the end of his life in 1858 he was more than £1 million in debt.

Stately 'Gossip'

The Vegetarian Huntsman

he eccentric nineteenth-century baronet Sir Charles Isham of Lamport Hall in Northamptonshire may have been a prominent vegetarian of his day but he was nonetheless a keen rider who went hunting on occasions. Sir Charles, who was a spiritualist, could also be rather absent-minded. One day he was spotted riding with the hunt when he stopped his mount just as man and beast were about to jump a large hedge. Sir Charles dismounted, went around the front of the horse for a few seconds, patted it knowingly, then remounted. Rider and horse then finally jumped the hedge. The 10th Baronet later explained to curious enquirers that he owned two fine horses, one headstrong, the other placid, and he wanted to be sure which one he was riding before he took on such a large hedge.

A Guided Bore

he impressive Arley Hall in Cheshire has been in the Ashbrook family for hundreds of years and is a popular venue for TV location shoots and weddings. In fact it has sometimes combined both, and has been the scene for two *Coronation Street* onscreen weddings in recent years. Further back in history, the future French emperor Napoleon III briefly lived at the hall.

Among many attractions, including some stunning gardens, Arley boasts a fine private chapel designed in the nineteenth century by the well-known Victorian architect Anthony Salvin. Understandably an earlier Lord Ashbrook was very proud of this chapel, and knew the history and significance of every square inch of the building. This came in useful one day when he was conducting a guided tour around the establishment. At the chapel Lord Ashbrook spared nothing in imparting to the gathered throng his unique knowledge of the structure and its merits. For some time his lordship expanded enthusiastically on the finer points of history and architecture until finally, and with a triumphant flourish, he finished his explanation. 'Any questions?' he asked enthusiastically.

The request was met with absolute silence as the group stood stunned by the volume of complex information they had just had imparted to them. The silence dragged on, with everyone present becoming embarrassed, not just for themselves but for their well-meaning guide. Finally, a hand at the back shot up.

Lord Ashbrook smiled with relief and instantly asked, 'Yes! How can I help you?'

'Excuse me,' said the man at the back. 'Can you tell me the quickest way to Northwich?'

Stately 'Gossip'

A Tangled Web

W illiam Cavendish, the 5th Duke of Devonshire, who was born in 1748, had a complicated private life. His first wife was Lady Georgiana Spencer, whose best friend was Lady Elizabeth Foster, the daughter of the 4th Earl of Bristol. But Lady Elizabeth was also the duke's mistress and the three of them lived together in London in a *ménage à trois* for some twenty years. After Georgiana's death the Duke married Lady Elizabeth. The Duke had three legitimate children by Georgiana, two illegitimate children by Elizabeth and also another child by yet another mistress, the daughter of a vicar. Just to add to the complication Georgiana also had a daughter Eliza by her lover the 2nd Earl Grey, who was later to become prime minister.

Green Park

T here was for a time at the end of the eighteenth century a fashion for women from the upper classes to visit a small farm in London on what is still known as Green Park. This farm was run by a Mrs Searle, and was in reality an idealised romantic version of what the well-to-do imagined a farm to be like, complete with a pretty little pond, some rambling roses and a few cows munching contentedly in a small field. On one occasion in 1793 no lesser person than the Prince of Wales arrived at the farm with his friend Lady Salisbury. While the prince looked on Lady Salisbury helped

Mrs Searle to milk the cows by hand. It was also the first occasion on which the prince met his future friend – and later enemy – George Bryan Brummell, better known as 'Beau', who was Mrs Searle's nephew and a handsome young lad of fifteen at the time.

Lost Loans

he naïve Lady Spencer seemed to sum up the old saying about having more money than sense when during a trip abroad she lent the then huge sum of £1,000 to the Queen of Naples. Though she wrote many letters requesting the repayment of the 'loan' the Queen of Naples did not deign to reply to the demands, apparently thinking it was the duty of the British aristocracy to fund foreign royalty. Instead she rather cheekily complained in a letter that Lady Spencer 'never wrote to her anymore'.

Her ladyship's response? 'I am very angry but it cannot be helped,' she told a friend in 1802. Needless to say Lady Spencer never saw a farthing of the money again. Yet she appears not to have learnt her lesson from this lost money. For shortly afterwards, on a visit to Paris, Lady Spencer lent another substantial sum to a female relative of Charles Talleyrand, the French foreign minister. Once again none of the money was ever paid back to her hapless ladyship.

Stately 'Gossip'

The Tragic Countess of Gaulstown

Of all the stories involving the stately homes of the British Isles, few can be as sad as that involving the beautiful yet tragic figure of the first Countess of Belvedere. Born Mary Molesworth, the daughter of Viscount Molesworth, she was 'persuaded' against her will to marry the unlovely Robert Rochfort in 1736. Rochfort later became the Earl of Belvedere and he and his wife had a number of children. But it seems the Earl was irrationally jealous from the start and feared that his wife had been or would be unfaithful. His fears seemed justified — at least in his eyes — with the discovery of some letters between Mary and one of his brothers that appeared to show some intimacy between them.

The Earl was outraged and so inflicted upon the Countess one of the cruellest and most heartless punishments imaginable. He had Mary effectively 'imprisoned' in the family seat at Gaulstown in Westmeath, Ireland. Here she was denied all access to her children, the rest of the family and the outside world; her only companions were some servants loyal to the Earl's wishes. Meanwhile the family resided at their new home at Belvedere. Even here the Earl's jealousy and envy drove him to the edge of madness, as he erected a structure between the house and nearby Tudenham House, where lived another brother with whom he had fallen out and whom the Earl believed lived in a grander house than his. This absurd construction has been known ever since as the 'Jealous Wall'.

Stately 'Gossip'

The inhuman treatment of Mary lasted for thirty years, from 1743 to 1774, until the death of her brute of a husband. She was released by her son, the new Earl of Belvedere, whom she had not seen for so many years. By all accounts the aged Countess cut a sorry figure, pale, gaunt and understandably bowed by the ordeal she had been forced to endure. Yet even as she lay dying a few years later, the Countess was unshaken in her certainty about one thing; she had never been unfaithful to her husband and determinedly protested her innocence on her death bed.

The Digger

James Clark, son of the late politician and brilliant diarist Alan Clark, once had something of a problem with caravans on the family's sizeable estates in Sutherland. The owners of caravans had a disconcerting habit of just parking on any land they could find for the night, irrespective of whether anyone owned it or not. Clark was becoming increasingly frustrated by the practice and decided that the issue called for a dramatic solution. His answer? He went out and bought a JCB digger.

That very evening he spotted yet another caravan parked on his land, the snoozing occupants —as usual — blissfully unaware that they were trespassing. This time James Clark resolved to teach the caravanning fraternity a lesson, so he got out his JCB and drove it to the spot where the caravan was parked. Then, and apparently without alerting the suspicion of anyone inside, Clark dug a deep ditch all around the offending vehicle.

The next morning Clark received a phone call from the sergeant at the local police station. 'Were you out last night Master James?' asked the policeman.

'No,' replied James Clark, 'what do you mean?'

The sergeant replied that there was a slight problem with a caravanner locally who had gone to sleep last night and awoken that morning to find he could not move his vehicle because there was now a huge trench around it. Did Master James know anything about it?

'How inconvenient for him,' replied James Clark calmly, adding that he knew nothing about the matter.

'Ok, well I just thought you might know something about it,' explained the sergeant.

'I'll certainly keep my eyes open,' offered James Clark.

'Thank you Master James,' replied the policeman. 'And can I suggest one thing?'

'Certainly Sergeant,' replied James Clark.

Stately 'Gossip'

'Maybe it would be a good idea to keep your JCB in the garage from now on,' said the sergeant.

Too Many Gardeners

Debts, especially those caused by gambling, have long hampered the owners of stately homes. During the Regency period, when gambling debts reached epidemic proportions, Lord Bessborough once had to pay gambling debts of more than £32,000 that had been racked up by his wife and sister-in-law. His solution? He decided to cut down on the number of gardeners they had at their country home. Apparently there were twelve of them, each costing half a guinea a week to employ.

First Impressions of Knole

The impressive National Trust property of Knole near Sevenoaks in Kent was the home of the Sackville family from 1603 and is the largest private house in England. Perhaps this explains why a royal personage in the form of Queen Mary, wife of George V, was particularly fond of the place; perhaps it reminded her of the spacious properties that the British monarchy has to live in.

One day in 1936, when the abdication crisis was still in full swing – her son Edward VIII was to abdicate in favour of her son George VI – Queen Mary decided to pay a visit to Knole. Doubtless it was a good chance to get out of the capital while the crisis ran its course. At the same time, and just a few miles away, a man called Robin Moore was staying with friends. Moore was a gifted mimic and one of his 'party tricks' was to impersonate Queen Mary, imagining what she might be saying to the Conservative Prime Minister Stanley Baldwin about the abdication crisis. Moore and his hosts were well aware that the Queen was a frequent visitor to Knole, and so some bright spark had the hilarious idea of getting Moore to dress up and imitate Queen Mary and visit Knole to see if owner Charles Sackville could spot the difference.

Accordingly Robin Moore put on the full regalia; clothes, hat, jewels – even some Pekinese dogs were found to accompany him to complete the authentic picture. And so the party set off to test the owner of Knole.

What they did not know, of course, was that the real Queen Mary was staying at Knole at the time. So it was with some horror – on both sides – that the Robin Moore version of Queen Mary strode majestically into Knole only to be confronted by the real thing. Alas, the discretion of the British royal family prevents us from knowing what the genuine Queen Mary thought and said about this monstrous impertinence as she was confronted with such an authentic lookalike. However, it does appear that the rather tense silence that surrounded the encounter was only broken when the impostor Queen Mary's Pekinese dogs decided to pick a fight with those belonging to the real Queen, and for a while bedlam broke out, during which the counterfeit Queen was able to beat a hasty and not entirely dignified retreat.

Situations Vacant

I n past centuries the position of mistress to a powerful nobleman or member of a royal family could be an attractive one. Some believed that it was preferable, indeed, to be a mistress rather than a wife. A few of the more sought-after mistresses could even name their, very extravagant, terms for such an arrangement. For example the newspapers in 1791 reported that the successful actress Mrs Jordan was demanding 'terms' to become the mistress of the Duke of Clarence. These conditions included a £1,200 a year annuity and that her children 'by all parties' should be provided for. This arrangement lasted for around twenty years.

The Disappearing Duke

T he 5th Duke of Portland, William John Cavendish Bentinck-Scott, was a curious man and led a curious life. Born in 1800, the Duke lived till he was seventy-nine, but never married and indeed there is no record of his ever having 'dated' a woman. This is almost certainly because of the crippling shyness from which the Duke suffered, a condition that was to shape his entire life. Though he became an MP as a young man and was a member of various regiments, Bentinck-Scott's introverted personality slowly led him to withdraw from the world and live as a recluse not just from society but from most of the people around him too.

To this end the Duke transformed Welbeck Abbey, the family estate in Nottinghamshire, from an 'ordinary' stately home into a stately hermit's cave. He removed the furniture from most of the house, choosing to live in just a few rooms in the west wing. The remaining rooms were painted pink and left empty save for a washbasin in each.

Next the Duke began his monumental feat of having built what was in effect a new home underground; it had a ballroom, a library, stables, kitchens, even a riding school — all of which were hacked out of rock and earth beneath. There was also a one and a half mile tunnel leading from below the house to the nearby railway station, so that the reclusive aristocrat could arrive at and leave his estate undetected. Meanwhile the tenants who worked on his estate were told to ignore the Duke if they ever saw him; indeed one workman placed under the same stricture was sacked on the spot for the heinous offence of saluting his lordship. However, in other respects the Duke was said to have been a good employer and ran his estates well.

Unsurprisingly, though, the house never echoed to the sounds of gaiety and laughter, and no guests were invited and no parties held. Even the vast ballroom the duke had ordered to be constructed underground was never used. Meanwhile his modest personal rooms were fitted with two letter boxes, one for outgoing and one for incoming correspondence to increase privacy from his own staff. Not even doctors were allowed to see him in person — a valet would take the duke's temperature and pass the thermometer to the doctor waiting on the other side of the door. On the rare occasions he did venture out — usually at night — the duke sometimes wore disguises and he had special blinds built on his coach to stop people looking in as he passed by.

All this curious behaviour attracted gossip and rumour, and there were wild reports that the Duke's hidden life was prompted by some hideous disfigurement. Yet contemporary reports suggest that the 5th Duke of Portland was an ordinary enough looking person. It seems instead that the Duke, who must have led a very lonely life, was introverted to the point of obsession and chose to live his life as privately and secretly as possible.

Young Love

Lord Erskine, the Lord Chancellor, caused a scandal in British society in the early nineteenth century by having the temerity to fall in love. After thirty-five years of marriage to his first wife, followed by thirteen years of living on his own after she died, he doubtless felt in need of love and affection in his later years. The problem was that his lordship fell in love with his young housekeeper.

Stately 'Gossip'

When the housekeeper, Sarah Buck, became pregnant with his child Lord Erskine honourably and bravely announced his intention to marry her and legitimise the baby. Unfortunately his sons from his first marriage feared they would lose their inheritance, and they tried to have Lord Erskine committed to an asylum to stop the marriage.

The lord and his young sweetheart were undeterred and fled north to Scotland with the sons in hot pursuit. Lord Erskine, as one might expect from a man with a cunning legal brain, outfoxed his children by disguising himself as an old woman and the happy couple were able to make it safely north of the border. Eventually the pair married in 1818. But the upset and scandal caused by the affair affected Erskine badly and he died just a few years later having had precious little time to enjoy the happiness that he had sought and fought for in his old age.

The Performing Butler

Wolterton Hall near Erpingham in North Norfolk was built by Thomas Ripley for Horatio Walpole, the younger brother of Robert Walpole, Britain's first Prime Minister. It is a quiet kind of place, with beautiful gardens, and has never been the centre of scandals. But it was the location for a curious dinner party in the 1920s given by its then owner the Earl of Orford, a descendant of the Walpole dynasty. The guest of honour was Stanley Baldwin, the Conservative Prime Minister, and his lordship had found out that the politician's favourite meal was roast suckling pig. Instructions were thus given to the kitchen to prepare this meal in honour of such a grand personage.

However the butler, who had not been with the family long, was unsure exactly how such a dish should be served. He asked Lady Orford for her advice and she informed him that it was served 'dressed up' with, for example, an apple in the mouth and fresh herbs behind the ears. The butler gratefully acknowledged her ladyship's advice and the final preparations for the meal were completed.

Imagine Lord and Lady Orford's surprise — not to say horror — however when the roast suckling pig was brought in. There indeed was the roasted animal on a fine silver platter; what really caught their appalled gaze was the sight of their new butler proudly carrying in the dish while holding a large apple in his mouth and sporting some fresh sprigs of parsley behind his ears.

It transpired that the butler, who had been recommended by an acquaintance, had indeed been in service as his references had stated. Alas that service had been as a stable boy, not serving in a house, and so the finer points of waiting at table were sadly lost on him.

Stately 'Gossip'

Marital Discord

T here have been few more outrageous and complicated scandals than that involving Lord Paget and Lady Charlotte Wellesley in 1809. When Lady Charlotte eloped with Lord Paget she was at the time married with four young children; her husband was the Duke of Wellington's brother Henry. Lord Paget was also married and was the father of no fewer than eight children. To excite matters further, Paget's wife was Lady Caroline Villiers, the daughter of Lady Jersey, an ex-mistress of the Prince Regent.

The family of each eloper blamed the other party for provoking this scandalous affair, and for months it was the talk of London society. The Duchess of Wellington was moved to describe the whole matter in forthright terms. 'What a complication of infamy and vice,' she wrote.

Amid all the accusation and counter-accusation of who did what to whom and when, there was at least something on which most people could agree; everyone felt very sorry for poor Lady Paget — the former Lady Caroline — who had been abandoned with her large brood of children by her feckless husband. Until, that is, there was yet another revelation in the sordid affair. It transpired that poor abandoned Lady Paget, far from being a blameless party, had herself been having an affair for years with the Duke of Argyll. Eventually there was a double divorce and Lady Charlotte married

Lord Paget, while Lady Paget wed her long-term lover and became the Duchess of Argyll.

The Affair of the Urn

There is an anonymous but apparently true story of how one house guest at a stately home in the north of England found himself the victim of his hosts' hospitality and the large and rambling nature of their house. The guest had been invited for the weekend and was both excited and nervous about the prospect of spending time in such exalted surrounds. As a result he decided to take a hip flask with him on the train journey to the house, and by the time he had arrived he was already a little merry.

Then during the course of a sumptuous dinner throughout which his wine and brandy glasses were kept constantly topped up, the nervous guest moved from being merry to becoming outright drunk. As a result the evening passed in something of a haze. In fact he barely remembered getting — or possibly being taken — to bed at all.

In the early hours the guest awoke, suddenly very aware that he needed to answer a call of nature, and urgently. The only question was, where? There were no en-suite guest rooms in that charming but un-modernised part of the house and the unfortunate man had neglected to locate the nearest convenience before indulging in the pleasures of the previous evening.

Stately 'Gossip'

Nervously he opened his door, padded into the corridor and looked for a sign of the WC. Alas all doors looked the same to him, and he could not risk stumbling in on one of his far more distinguished fellow guests in their sleep. Instead he crept downstairs and searched along the ground floor corridors for signs of the loo. Here, too, he drew a blank and could find no sign of the littlest room, just huge dining rooms and drawing rooms. By now his quest was more urgent than ever, and so in desperation he looked around for something that could provide him with temporary relief. His eyes alighted upon one of the house's Grecian urns and without a moment's further hesitation he settled down on it and let nature take its course.

As he finally made his way upstairs, much relieved, he mentally resolved to wake early and come downstairs to dispose of the incriminating evidence before anyone could detect what had happened. Alas the night's exertions had taken their toll, and by the time the guest awoke from his slumbers the morning had advanced well past ten o'clock and the household and fellow guests were wide awake and up and about.

All the guest could do was wait and hope, while the hours ticked by, that his 'crime' would go unnoticed. Sadly, this proved a forlorn hope. For it became apparent to the household and guests alike that there was a powerful and unpleasant odour making its way through the ground floor of the stately home, though its exact source was a mystery. As the day wore on the stench became worse and worse, and soon guests were starting to make unscheduled plans to leave that evening rather than stay another night. Our unfortunate guest, seizing this opportunity, also invented a pressing engagement 'in town' and left with the other visitors fleeing from that awful odour.

Back in London our man congratulated himself on his good fortune. True, the weekend had been interrupted, but at least he had managed to escape the blame for his unfortunate nighttime escapade. Or so, at least, he thought. The next morning he received a telegram that made his face go white and his knees tremble with fear. It had been sent by his hosts of the previous weekend and read simply, 'WE KNOW YOU DID IT BUT WHERE?'

The Royal Duke's Mistress

I n 1805 the Duke of York met a pretty young actress by the name of Mary Anne Clarke and was so smitten with her charms that he very soon had her installed as his mistress. She was set up in a nice house in Mayfair in London, and was allowed to spend £2,000 on refurbishing it. Mary Anne was also given a generous £1,000 a year allowance and handed the use of a house in the country as well. This was so she could meet her royal paramour even while he was at Oatlands Park , the wonderful Surrey mansion where he lived with the Duchess of York, the daughter of the King of Prussia. But even this excellent arrangement seems not to have been able to satisfy Mary Anne's demand for luxuries and she was soon paying out far more on dresses and lavish entertaining and gifts that she appeared to be 'earning'. People were puzzled; even by the standards of a well-connected mistress of the day her expenditure seemed excessive.

Then in 1809 it all became clear. To make extra money Mary Anne had been selling commissions in the army. The Duke was commander-in-chief of the armed forces and as such was ultimately responsible for all promotions and appointments. There was a waiting list for commissions and thanks to the laws of supply and demand there was therefore a price on various types of commission; for example to get a commission as a major could set a person back as much as £2,600. It seems the resourceful Mary Anne had been discreetly adding a few names to the Duke's list of impending commissions in return for a large fee from the would-be officers. The issue became a huge scandal and was eventually investigated by members of the House of Commons. Ultimately there was no definite proof that the Duke knew what his mistress had been doing and he was acquitted by the Commons.

Yet shaken by the scandal the Duke felt obliged to resign as commander-in-chief while Mary Anne Clarke briefly became a minor celebrity of the day.

Stately 'Gossip'

Blunder at Blakeston Castle

Some members of the upper classes show remarkable trust in their staff, even those hired on a whim abroad and charged with something as important as building a new home for them. Such was the case with baronet Sir Robert Blakeston, who decided to create a splendid new family pile called Blakeston Castle. Not for Sir Robert a modest little country mansion, either; he wanted a full-on castle built in the latest Italian style of the mid-nineteenth century. This meant of course that the Baronet needed to commission a genuine Italian architect to do the work.

Not knowing many of these personally, Sir Robert sensibly – or so it seemed – engaged an agent in Venice to do the hiring for him. The agent duly contacted and commissioned a respected Italian architect, Guido Spinolini, as Sir Robert had bidden him. There was just one snag. Somehow the agent had got his names a little confused and did not hire *Guido* Spinolini, but somehow managed to commission his brother – also a Spinolini – to do the work.

Now this brother, whose first name, alas, has not survived the telling of the tale, was delighted to be commissioned for such a prestigious undertaking. The problem was that far from being an architect, this Signor Spinolini lived in a rather seedy part of Venice, spoke little or no English and ran a pawnshop. The Italian, of course, was not going to look this particular gift horse in the mouth and as Sir Robert was none the wiser, the pawnshop owner eagerly travelled to England to take up the commission. Here Signor Spinolini was in luck. An enthusiastic Sir Robert had done much of the preparation work himself, including the making of detailed drawings, and really just needed the architect to confirm the Baronet's intentions and to add his own inimitable, authentic Italian touch to the project.

So after a few discussions with Signor Spinolini about the size of certain rooms and features, Sir Robert set off on a lengthy tour of the East feeling sure that upon his return he would be the proud owner of a new and magnificent castle. Instead when, nearly a year later, Sir Robert got back to Blakeston he found a massive half-finished shell of a building site. It seems that the architect had indeed added his Italian 'touch'; for, coming from the continent, the pawnshop owner-turned architect had used metres for the dimensions rather than the feet indicated by Sir Robert. The result was a vast sprawling monstrosity of a building. Had it ever been completed it would have rivalled the palace at Versailles in scale.

Unsurprisingly the ill-fated construction was pulled down just thirty years later.

Stately 'Gossip'

The Duchess of York

uring the Regency the Duke and Duchess of York had their country home at Oatlands Park, a delightful house near Weybridge in Surrey that is now a splendid hotel. Here the somewhat eccentric Duchess displayed her passionate love of animals. As well as one hundred dogs, she kept monkeys and tame kangaroos. There was also an aviary that contained parrots, macaws and even eagles, while the sentimental duchess also had constructed a dog cemetery for her favourite hounds to be put to rest in when they died.

Perhaps the energy and time required in looking after this vast menagerie explains why one frequent visitor to the house for weekend parties described Oatlands at the time as the 'worst managed establishment in England'. The Duchess certainly behaved oddly at times. She rarely went to bed, certainly not at night, and was often to be seen roaming around the massive house or the gardens in the early hours of the morning, usually accompanied by some of her beloved dogs. She took breakfast alone at three o'clock in the morning and often only met up with her guests at dinner, preferring the company of the animals the rest of the time.

Another problem was a lack of money; despite handsome allowances the Duke and Duchess spent it extravagantly. Once the Duchess was hosting a large party and wanted to prolong the entertainment for a day or so when they hit a snag – there was suddenly no water in the house. The supply pipes had become blocked with sand and worse still, the workmen had refused to clear them because they had not been paid for earlier work. The Duchess pleaded that the work had to be carried out, and reluctantly it was, but when the bill was presented she was embarrassed to find that her household steward had no funds with which to pay for it. Finally and to everyone's embarrassment the Duke was prevailed upon to find some cash.

Yet despite these peculiar habits and financial mishaps the Duchess was generally agreed to be a very popular hostess both with guests and her staff, and was also noted for her work in helping the poor and needy. So popular was she in fact that after her death local people built a memorial for her at Monument Hill in Weybridge.

Bad Timing

One day in the late 1960s a young man was invited to a weekend house party in Wiltshire at the imposing Wilton House, the family home of the Earls of Pembroke which is nearly 500 years old. However, the young guest was less interested in the architectural magnificence of this great building than the fact that an attractive fellow guest had suggested to him that they should spend the weekend getting to know each other intimately. On one point, however, she was adamant; before this blissful relationship could commence the young man had to produce some form of contraception.

Stately 'Gossip'

Buoyed by the prospect of a weekend with such a charming companion, the young man set off to the nearby shops with a spring in his step. But there was a problem. It was already getting late on Friday and the shops, and worst of all the chemist, were shut. Wherever he looked it was the same story. At last, in desperation, and using some lateral thinking, the young guest spotted a barber's shop. Though it was closed he managed to attract the attention of the owner, a middle-aged man with the air of someone far older. As casually as he could, the young man asked in time-honoured fashion whether the barber sold 'something for the weekend'. After what seemed like an interminable pause the barber replied loftily that he was 'not in that kind of business' and shut the door on him.

With that final failure, the young man knew his weekend's amorous activities were doomed, but as he walked disconsolately back to Wilton House he at least comforted himself with the thought that it was still a fine place in which to spend a weekend eating and drinking. Or at least so he thought. Alas, when he got back he found his luggage had been put outside the house and on enquiring why, was told by the butler that his hosts wished him to return to London that evening. It seems his attempts to purchase a condom had aroused the suspicion of the locals, and the local bobby had taken it upon himself to phone Wilton House to warn the household of the young man's activities and his obvious amorous intentions.

Stately 'Gossip'

Hats Off

According to traditional accounts, the ancient Irish noblemen known as the Barons of Kingsale had acquired the right to appear in the presence of a British monarch without removing their hats. Though some scholars doubt the authenticity of the tale, this right is said to stretch back to the days of King John in the early thirteenth century. (Others claim it was given by Henry VIII, who was scared of catching ringworm from the then Baron Kingsale and so let him keep his hat on.) In any case, it was a right that went untested for centuries, indeed until the nineteenth century when the 32nd Baron, Michael William de Courcy, bravely tried to resurrect the custom upon meeting Queen Victoria. The Baron told the Queen he meant no disrespect, but was simply asserting his ancient right. Fixing him with a deadly stare, the Queen retorted, 'It might be your right to keep your hat on before the monarch but I am a lady too. Take it off at once.'

The crestfallen Baron apparently did as he was told.

Cardigan's Uniforms

The much-maligned Lord Cardigan, who is usually and unfairly blamed for the disastrous Charge of the Light Brigade in the Valley of Balaclava in 1854, was always keen that his men looked their best. He sent the officers of the regiment that he commanded — the 11th Light Dragoons — to the best tailors in

London to get them kitted out in the smartest of uniforms. He then paid the bill out of his own pocket.

Cardigan, whose family lived at Deene Park in Northamptonshire, certainly had an interesting life. His first marriage was so unhappy that when his wife ran off with a lover he thanked his rival for doing him 'the greatest service that one man can render to another'.

Stately Rivalry

During the 1960s the opening up of stately homes to the public was not just a necessity for many owners, but it was also big business. It was therefore important to know what one's 'rivals' at other magnificent piles were offering their customers. To this end Lord Bath decided to check out the opposition at Lord Montagu's place at Beaulieu, which is splendidly situated in the New Forest in Hampshire. Lord Bath tried to visit the home incognito several times, posing as a paying guest, but could never get past the experienced woman at the admissions desk who, much to his chagrin, always recognised his lordship. She would inform Lord Montagu who would then pop out for a chat with the 'spy' from Longleat. 'I can never get past that woman without her noticing!' Lord Bath would exclaim in frustration each time he failed to see round Beaulieu.

This may of course have had something to do with the fact that his lordship never made any attempt to disguise himself and indeed always wore a distinctive red-spotted handkerchief in his breast pocket.

The Hibernating Peer

A certain Lord North, a descendant of the British prime minister of the same name, the one often blamed for the loss of the American colonies in the eighteenth century, had just got married. Ironically, perhaps, his new bride was an American. At any rate this Lord North had a surprise in store for his new wife, a habit he had neglected to warn her about — he hibernated each winter.

The aristocrat apparently never stirred from his bedroom from October until mid-March, not unless the weather was particularly agreeable. He even had a special hole cut in a large wooden dining table so he could still enjoy the company of guests for dinner without leaving the comfort of his bed. Lord North told his bemused wife that hibernation had been a family trait ever since his ancestor 'lost' the colonies.

Happenings at Harewood

Harewood House near Leeds is one of the ten Treasure Houses of England and thus is not only a magnificent building but also houses some important collections, notably of Chippendale furniture. As such its security under the watchful gaze of the 7th Earl of Harewood and his family is of the highest standard. However, it was not always quite so assured. Decades ago, when security issues at such houses were only just beginning to be addressed, a manager at Harewood decided to put the staff's alertness to the test. To this end the manager constructed a dummy bomb and hid it behind a radiator in a quiet part of the house. The staff were then given a talk on the importance of security and told to conduct a thorough search of the whole establishment. To the manager's horror, the search failed to discover the makeshift 'bomb'; indeed it was not found until three days later when a member of staff chanced upon it by accident.

The security-minded manager decided to have another attempt. This time he went to a nearby village telephone box and, disguising his voice, rang the house. 'I have a warning for you,' said the manager in his strange voice when the receptionist answered the call. 'There's a bomb at the house.'

'I beg your pardon,' replied the receptionist. 'Would you mind repeating that?'

The manager persevered. 'I said there's a BOMB in the house.'

'Is there?' responded the receptionist. 'Thank you very much.' At which she promptly hung up.

Still, despite the receptionist's less than urgent reaction, the manager consoled himself with the thought that at least he had got his message across and he hurried back to the house to observe how the staff reacted to this chilling warning.

Unfortunately, he discovered there had been no reaction. Instead he found the receptionist quietly reading a magazine.

Astonished, the manager demanded: 'Did you not receive a telephone call a short time ago?'

'Yes,' replied the receptionist calmly. 'There was someone who kept on repeating, "There's a bomb in the house".'

'And . . .?' said the manager.

'Well he didn't leave his name,' replied the receptionist, gloriously missing the point. 'So I'm afraid I couldn't tell you who it was.'

The Noble Outlaw

The fifteenth-century nobleman Henry, the 11th Lord Clifford, later the Earl of Cumberland, was a pleasure-seeking young man who needed money to fund his extravagance.

Unfortunately he was on poor terms with his father and so had little money of his own. His solution to this dilemma may seem a little drastic by today's standards; he gathered a group of ruthless followers and turned into an outlaw, terrorising the countryside and causing mayhem at religious houses. This peculiar way for an aristocrat to behave does not seem to have harmed his advancement too much, however. Later in life, when he had calmed down, Henry was made a Knight of the Garter.

Lord Clifford's father also had a curious life. Known as the 'Shepherd Earl', he lived as a herdsman for twenty-five years to escape the Yorkists during the Wars of the Roses. When he emerged from hiding under the reign of Henry VII he was apparently illiterate, though later in life he retired from public life to devote himself to the study of astronomy.

Raise a Glass

Few people enjoyed the good life more than General Sir John Irwin. When he was Lord Lieutenant of Ireland in 1781 he had made a huge dessert that was an exact replica of the fortress of Gibraltar; it even had cannons that fired sugar plums at the dining room wall.

Dessert was not his only love. The King once said to him, 'Sir John, they tell me that you love a glass of wine!'

Stately 'Gossip'

Sir John protested that the King's informants, whoever they were, had badly misrepresented him. 'They should have said a bottle!' he said with a smile.

The Tranby Croft Scandal

Gambling at house parties at stately homes was not always just a question of money, but of honour too. In 1890 the Prince of Wales, 'Bertie', the future Edward VII, was on a trip to the north of England to visit Doncaster Races. Before the races he had been staying at a grand if inelegant home called Tranby Croft, owned by a wealthy shipbuilder by the name of Arthur Wilson. As was his custom the Prince wanted to play the card game baccarat, and as usual he played for money (not usually his own).

Among the party was Sir William Gordon Cumming of Altyre, 4th Baronet, and a veteran of the Zulu War of 1879. He was a man of honour but also known as a fairly sharp card player. Play was continuing happily enough until the unimaginable happened. Sir William, a gentleman and baronet, was suddenly and abruptly accused of cheating by a fellow player. This accusation was bad enough for any gentleman or titled person; but for a friend of the Prince and honoured military veteran it was a disgrace. What seems to have happened next was that, after lengthy deliberation between the other players, a deal was struck to extricate everyone from this delicate and potentially explosive situation. Sir William would agree to sign a piece of paper stating that he would never play cards again; while his fellow players pledged solemnly never to speak publicly of the affair and to keep it a secret. That way honour would be maintained on all sides.

Perhaps inevitably the story leaked out, some say via Bertie's mistress Daisy, Lady 'babbling' Brooke who was known for her love of gossip. The resulting publicity now meant that Sir William's good standing was lowered in the eyes of polite society, and he felt obliged to sue a number of his fellow players for slander. Sir William did not sue the Prince of Wales, but the future king was called as a witness to the case and inevitably the affair became a huge scandal. Much of public opinion was on the side of Sir William and to this day it is still not entirely clear whether this wealthy man actually did cheat, and if so why.

Not surprisingly, and not for the first time in his colourful life, the Prince of Wales came in for some heavy criticism both for being involved in such an unsavoury affair, and also for indulging in card playing and gambling at all. Sir William lost his legal action, and though he may have won something of a victory in the court of ordinary public opinion, he nonetheless had to 'retire' from society and henceforth spent much of the rest of his life at the family estates at Gordonstoun, better known now as the location for the school where a later Prince of Wales – Prince Charles – was educated.

Stately 'Gossip'

Long-living Lord

The first Earl of Bathurst seemed to have learnt the secret of growing old. He reached the very decent age of ninety-one in 1775 despite, or because of, his habit of riding for two hours before dinner every day and then polishing off a whole bottle of claret after the meal. His doctor once told him that unless he stopped drinking so much he would die within seven years; that advice was given when Lord Bathurst was still in his forties.

The Count and the Writ

One of the constant problems befalling many members of the aristocracy in Britain is falling into debt, and the never-ending battles caused by money – or lack of it.

This dilemma also applied to members of the French nobility staying in Britain. Alfred Guillaume Gabriel, Count d'Orsay, the son of a Bonapartist general and a dandy, was part of the smart set in London in the 1830s and 1840s and was regarded as an authority on matters of taste in society. As a profligate spender of money and responsible for growing debts, he also needed to become an expert on English law as it related to debtors. At his home he ensured that two huge dogs kept out unwelcome visitors, so that the Count could avoid anyone serving a writ for arrest for debts on him. One afternoon, however, a resourceful bailiff managed to slip into the house disguised as an errand boy and came across a surprised Count in his dressing room. The bailiff was about to serve the writ but the elegant Count asked if he could at least refrain from doing the inevitable deed while he dressed himself. For nearly an hour the bailiff waited patiently, fascinated by the dandy's exquisite and complicated dressing routine. Then as the Count finally finished, the bailiff rose from his chair to serve the writ.

The Count however knew exactly what he had been doing and triumphantly pointed out of the window, noting to the bailiff that dusk had now fallen. As the official was reminded, one of the peculiarities of the law at that time was that no such writ could be served between sunset and sunrise. The crestfallen and out-witted official was courteously invited to leave, and the Count survived to fight another day.

Dashwood of West Wycombe

One of the most notorious noblemen of his or any generation was Sir Francis Dashwood, the eighteenth-century bon viveur who lived at West Wycombe Park in Buckinghamshire. Throughout his action-packed life Sir Thomas was associated with the occult and was regarded by some as a devil-worshipper – though the truth is he was probably simply a pagan at heart who worshipped the old gods revered by the ancient Greeks and Romans.

Stately 'Gossip'

One of the sources of the rumours was his secretive club 'The Order of the Friars of St Francis of Wycombe' better known to many as the 'Hellfire Club'. This club, which originally met at West Wycombe Park, was made up of some of the most influential people of the day and was said to have created secret and highly-suggestive rituals that they carried out at night at a disused monastery a few miles from West Wycombe. All the records of the club's events and ceremonies were destroyed by its secretary at the end of his life. But there were rumors of sexual practices during ceremonies to the old gods, and scandalous reports that aristocratic ladies volunteered to take part in one ritual in which they assumed the role of a goddess lying naked on a makeshift altar.

None of this unusual background seems to have affected the public life of Sir Francis, who became an MP, briefly and unsuccessfully Chancellor of the Exchequer and ultimately Paymaster General in 1766 – having been appointed by no less a politician than William Pitt. Sir Francis also had a prodigious sexual appetite and was said by a contemporary to have had 'the staying power of a stallion and the impetuosity of a bull'. It has even been suggested that he had a brief liaison with the Russian Tsarina, Anna Ivanovna, on a visit to St. Petersburg in 1733.

Yet this intriguing character had many sides to him: he was responsible for having designed the sumptuous gardens at West Wycombe Park that can still be visited today and later in life collaborated with Benjamin Franklin on a revised edition of the *Book of Common Prayer* for the Church of England.

The Duchess and the Queen

arah Jennings, who was born in 1660, became the first Duchess of Marlborough and for a while was recognised as being one of the most powerful women in the land. She also lived at the truly glorious Blenheim Palace. Yet despite this power and the glittering lifestyle that went with it, the Duchess also had a very cautious approach to money; it was even said that she saved on ink by not using full stops or dotting her i's.

The duchess gained much notoriety in her lifetime – and even more ever since – for her close relationship with Queen Anne. It has been suggested that the friends had a sexual relationship; while no hard evidence of this has ever been produced, they certainly were very close. This closeness ended however when the Queen in turn became friends with one of Sarah's cousins, Abigail Hill, and the spurned Duchess became a critic of the Queen until the latter's death in 1714.

Stately 'Gossip'

The Lost Leg of Plas Newydd

he National Trust-owned property of Plas Newydd in North Wales is set in a breathtaking location with wonderful views of Snowdonia. It was also the ancestral home of one of the most remarkable British army officers who ever fought for his country. Henry Paget, or Lord Uxbridge as he then was, was in charge of the cavalry at the Battle of Waterloo and was one of the Duke of Wellington's key men – even though he had caused a scandal through his elopement with the wife of Wellington's brother Henry. Paget had already enjoyed a glittering career as a cavalry officer and as this battle drew to its dramatic conclusion it seemed that the handsome young peer had come through yet another great confrontation unscathed. Yet with victory already in sight, one of the last French cannon fusillades rang out and shrapnel from a cannon shot hit the aristocrat's right leg as he watched the battle on his horse. The exchange that now followed between the wounded Paget and the Duke of Wellington must count as one of the most remarkable conversations in military history.

'By God, I've lost my leg,' remarked Lord Uxbridge to his commander-in-chief.

The Iron Duke briefly glanced down at Paget's mangled leg before looking back up again at the French lines, 'By God sir, so you have,' he commented.

In fact Paget had been hit on the right knee and his leg was so badly injured it had to be amputated, though as there was no anaesthetic available the officer simply had to bite on a cork while the operation was performed. Still as Paget noted, who would not lose a leg for such a victory as theirs over Napoleon?

The offending limb was later buried near an inn at Waterloo with an inscription over it which read,

> Here lies the Marquess of Anglesey's leg
> Pray for the rest of his body we beg.

The Marquess of Anglesey was the title bestowed on Paget by a grateful nation; and fortunately the peer enjoyed forty more years of life in which to savour the honour, and to appreciate his eighteen children and seventy-three grandchildren. Meanwhile Paget's artificial leg, plus a pair of muddy Hussar trousers from the battlefield, can still be seen at Plas Newydd, a reminder of one of the more unusual glimpses into the mindset and sang froid of the British aristocracy.

The Real Lord Montagu

After a gathering of stately home owners in central London, the Duke of Bedford and a friend decided to hail a taxi to take them to their destination. Once the two men were in the car, the taxi driver peered in the mirror at the Duke and said, 'Excuse me guv, but don't I know your face?'

Stately 'Gossip'

The Duke replied, naturally enough: 'I'm Bedford, from Woburn.'

'That's a good one, guv,' said the taxi driver. 'Well if you're the Duke of Bedford then I'm Lord Montagu!'

At this the Duke's companion tapped the driver on the shoulder and said: 'Excuse me, but *I'm* Lord Montagu!'

The Earl and the Sovereign

The splendid fourteenth-century Naworth Castle in Cumbria is still the home of the Earls of Carlisle, whose family name is Howard. The 9th Earl, George, who died in 1911, was a talented painter and spent much of his time absorbed in his art while his strong-minded wife Rosalind looked after the castle and estates.

George had his own studio, a stone building, where he used to spend hour after hour painting. One day the occupants of a horse-drawn wagon pulled up, with a view to looking around the castle. Disturbed by the commotion George came out, very artistic in his old painting clothes, and was asked somewhat unnecessarily, 'Are you the painter?'

When the Earl, who was a little nonplussed at all this, agreed that, yes, he was, he was then asked if he would mind holding the horses. 'While we look around the castle,' explained one of the party pleasantly.

For reasons unknown the Earl agreed and held on to the horses while the group set off to explore the magnificent building. Admittedly after a while the Earl got bored and tied the horses up, but he reappeared on the spot just in time to see the visitors returning. They thanked him profusely for his help and then tipped him a gold sovereign for his efforts, before moving off apparently none the wiser as to their horse attendant's true identity.

His family later said it was the only occasion in his life on which the 9th Earl of Carlisle ever got paid for doing a job.

The Singing Nun

In 1908 the Countess of Cardigan scandalised villagers near her home at Deene Park in Northamptonshire by going out shooting while wearing a kilt and leaving her knees bare. She was something of a character right into old age. Sometimes she would wear her late husband's military uniform, on other occasions she wore full evening dress on fine summer afternoons. She continued to sing and dance at parties until she was in her eighties. The Countess once even caused a female guest to faint at one of her parties when she burst into the event dressed as a nun and singing 'Ave Maria' at the top of her voice.

Stately 'Gossip'

Second Thoughts

A rather grand and elegant wife of a lord decided to sack her parlour maid, whom she felt was not up to the job, though she was, in all honesty, slightly jealous of the girl's extremely pretty looks. Her ladyship told the girl, who listened to her marching orders in complete silence.

But once her mistress had finished the confident young maid said, 'Now that I have been dismissed I feel free to speak my mind. I should tell you that his lordship has often had occasion to tell me that I am a better housekeeper than you and a far better cook!' She paused for a second and then added: 'And that I'm much better in bed than you are!'

Her ladyship sat down quickly to calm herself. 'Good heavens,' she said in a hurt voice. 'Did my husband *really* say all that?'

'No,' said the maid with a smile. 'The chauffeur did.'

Noblesse Oblige

Those born to high positions have an easy superiority which elevates them effortlessly above the common herd. Edward VII was said to be such a man. During his long spell as Prince of Wales he impressed an American guest at a reception they attended by his easy-going manner. 'You know, he treated me as an equal,' remarked the American afterwards, more than favourably disposed towards the idea of royalty.

'Yes.' replied the English courtier to whom he made the remark, 'His Royal Highness is always ready to forget his rank – as long as everyone else remembers it.'

Of course, the Prince of Wales was no mean host himself. It is said that guests at Sandringham weekend parties would be weighed on their arrival and departure. Any who failed to put on a pound or two had to answer to His Royal Highness himself.

Guests who were unable to accept his hospitality had their own way of conveying their apologies. One of his closest friends, Lord Charles Beresford, once declined an invitation to dine with him by sending a telegram that purportedly read, 'VERY SORRY CAN'T COME LIE FOLLOWS IN POST'.

Manners Maketh Royalty

In spite of her reputation for unbending propriety, Queen Victoria was perfectly capable of displaying the best of good manners when the occasion demanded. Dining in state during the visit of an eastern potentate the Queen noticed her guest of honour cheerfully sipping water from his finger-bowl. Without further ado and to spare her guest any embarrassment at his minor *faux pas*, the Queen took up her own finger-bowl and followed his example.

Effortless One-upmanship

T he attention the great and the good pay to the hospitality they show towards guests says much about the care they take over the finer things in life. This was certainly the case in the anecdote told of the carefree opulence displayed by the Rothschild family, notably at their Buckinghamshire seat at Waddesden Manor, which is now in the care of the National Trust.

H.H. Asquith, then serving as Prime Minister, was staying at Waddesden one weekend and, as teatime approached, was offered some refreshment by the butler. 'Tea, coffee, or a peach from the wall, sir?'

'Tea, please,' answered Asquith.

'China, Indian or Ceylon, sir?'

'China, please.'

'Lemon, milk or cream, sir?'

'Milk, please.'

'Jersey, Hereford or Shorthorn, sir?'

Money Talks

rom the days of hansom cabs comes a story of Lord Rothschild himself on the occasion that he hired a cab to take him home one evening. Alighting at the door of his London town house he paid the cabby and presented him with what he thought was a perfectly reasonable tip. The cabby thought otherwise, and after pocketing the coin rather disdainfully informed his fare, 'I've often driven your lordship's son home and he always gives me a good deal more than you've done.'

'I daresay he does,' answered Lord Rothschild. 'But then, you see, he has got a rich father: I haven't!'

Simply a Question of Taste

relatively young peer of the realm, who had already established a respectable reputation for his excellent wine cellar, gave a dinner party after a day's hunting to a large group of associates that included many guests far older than he. When the port was served he noticed one of the company, who was also well known for his knowledge of wines, nosing and examining the colour of his drink with an air of considerable doubt. His young host asked if anything was the matter, to which the older man answered that he thought the port was corked.

At this cue the other diners ceased sipping their glasses and confirmed to a man that indeed the port was corked.

Their host summoned his butler and asked him to fetch the other decanter.

This was duly brought, along with fresh glasses, and was passed round. One sip was enough to confirm that this was definitely superior. The young master of the house smiled reassuringly and asked his butler, 'Which bottle of port is this?'

'It's the other half of the magnum, my lord,' he replied.

I'm All Right, Jacques

On occasions it was necessary for considerate employers to advance their servants clothes, which it was generally accepted they would inherit when their employers had finished with them. Lieutenant-Colonel Jacques Balsan, who married Consuelo Vanderbilt after her divorce from the 9th Duke of Marlborough, had to help his valet out of a tight spot while they were visiting Blenheim Palace on one occasion. His man complained that other valets staying there were scornful of his blue serge suit, so to help him keep up appearances in the servants' quarters, Balsan had to lend him a dinner jacket.

If Music be the Food of . . .?

efined, artistic temperaments are not infrequently tinged with a degree of harmless eccentricity that also helps to set apart those of higher station. Such a man was John Christie, founder of the Glyndebourne Festival Opera. Sixteen years as a master at Eton had left him with a passion for milk puddings (he'd been known to wolf down half a dozen helpings of tapioca at a sitting) and a love of English literature. This he used to share with the troops in the trenches of the Great War, reading extracts from such enduring favourites as Spenser's *Faerie Queene* and holding a question period at the end of each session.

Christie had an impish sense of fun that impelled him to write letters to *The Times* inspired by objects that attracted his curiosity. One was a kipper he'd just consumed for breakfast, which prompted the enquiry whether or not kippers were 'for want of a better term . . . left-handed', based on Christie's careful observation that some kippers had backbones on one side of their body, others backbones on the other side.

His sense of dress was unconventional too. In spite of owning 132 pairs of socks and 110 shirts at one time, he frequently teamed the white tie of his evening dress with a pair of well-worn tennis shoes. He also developed a great enthusiasm for lederhosen, and visitors to Glyndebourne in the summer of 1933, when this sartorial phase reached its peak, were expected to appear similarly attired.

John Christie was at ease in any society. Sitting next to the Queen at dinner once he removed his glass eye and polished it assiduously in his handkerchief for a minute or two before popping it back in and asking Her Majesty, 'In straight, Ma'am?' On the other hand he made it a habit always to travel third class whenever he took a train journey.

His attitude to music was less unconventional and his devotion to the work of Mozart was evident from the Glyndebourne repertoire. Contemporary operas, though occasionally performed, were greeted with some reluctance – and not by Christie alone. Patrons wandering through the gardens during an interval in Hans Werner Henze's *Elegy For Young Lovers* came across Christie, an old man by this time, looking across the fields. 'Do you see those cows off in the distance?' Christie asked. 'Well, when we do Mozart, they are always right here.'